WESTMAR COLLEGE LIBRARY

W9-BXO-848

TWENTIETH CENTURY VIEWS

The aim of this series is to present the best in contemporary critical opinion on major authors, providing a twentieth century perspective on their changing status in an era of profound revaluation.

Maynard Mack, *Series Editor*
Yale University

THE MODERN
AMERICAN THEATER

THE MODERN AMERICAN THEATER

A COLLECTION OF CRITICAL ESSAYS

Edited by

Alvin B. Kernan

Prentice-Hall, Inc. *Englewood Cliffs, N.J.*

A SPECTRUM BOOK

792.0973
K 38
PN
2266
.K38

Copyright © 1967 by Prentice-Hall, Inc., *Englewood Cliffs, New Jersey*. A SPECTRUM BOOK. All rights reserved. No part of this book may be reproduced in any form or by any means without permission in writing from the publisher. *Library of Congress Catalog Card Number 67-25930*. Printed in the United States of America.

Current printing (last number):

10 9 8 7 6 5 4 3 2 1

Contents

PART FOUR—The Problems

Introduction

by Alvin B. Kernan

"Exult each patriot heart, this night is shewn a
piece which we may fairly call our own."

> (Prologue to Royall
> Tyler's *The Contrast*,
> 1787, the first play
> written by an Ameri-
> can and produced by
> professionals)

These high hopes voiced on the first night of the American
theater have not been borne out. Although we have produced during our relatively short national history a reasonable number of
first-rate poets and novelists, who have brought the peculiar quality
of the American experience into focus and raised it to the level of
great literature, we have had only a very few plays comparable to
our best novels and poetry. For myself, I would list only *The Skin
of Our Teeth, A Long Day's Journey Into Night, Death of A Salesman, A Streetcar Named Desire,* and—somewhat more hesitantly
—*Zoo Story.* Each of these has, of course, its violent critics; and
there are many whose judgment I respect who would deny that
some or any of them can rightly be termed great drama.

That we have never created a theater that speaks for us as, say, the
theater of Corneille, Racine, and Molière spoke for the France of
Louis XIV, puzzles us in the same way that the educated Roman
may have been puzzled when he compared Plautus, Terence, and
Seneca with Aristophanes, Aeschylus, and Sophocles. After all, we
have been busy theatrically. Enormous amounts of money from individual backers, from foundations, and from government have
gone into theaters to support many types of plays. Nor has money
been lacking for numerous conferences on theater and the publication of an endless outpouring of books and articles that deal with

things theatrical. There are schools—supported to some degree by contributions from a variety of sources—for actors, playwrights, and directors. In numerous universities and colleges both the classical and the modern drama are taught to large numbers of students who will hopefully become, if not the perfect audience, at least a more enlightened one than the theater has ever known. Above all, there is a vast network of theaters. Leaving aside television and the movies, which also to some degree generate and train an audience for the theater, our theaters extend to and beyond the far horizon. There is Broadway, and then Off-Broadway, and beyond it Off-Off-Broadway, and off that even the various underground theaters, the Kinetic Theater, the Ray-Gun Theater, the Theater of Chance. There are the various civic theaters—both public and private—summer stock, festival theaters, university theaters, and children's theaters. Theaters devoted to staging the work of one man, theaters that produce passion plays, and theaters that offer epic regional dramas.

Without question a great deal more could be done to "support" —this key term in our jargon has an unintended ominous quality, as if the thing supported could not stand by itself—the American theater and to train people for the various theatrical professions. But at the same time it is perfectly apparent that there is an enormous amount of theatrical activity in this country—probably more than there has ever been in any one place at one time—and, while the conditions may not be ideal, there is a great deal of opportunity for playwrights, actors, directors, and other technicians to learn and practice their trades.

If this is so, and the case seems undeniable, why have we produced so little great drama? Why have we not yet created a true theatrical tradition that is nourished by the playwrights and that nourishes them in turn? The answers to these questions have been many, most of them no doubt true. One involves the enormous costs of mounting a Broadway production, which insures that only a play appealing to the most common appetite can succeed; then there are the lures of the Bitch-Goddess Success, the patron of Hollywood and television, which pervert the talents of playwrights and actors. There are the labor unions, the star system, the ticket-scalpers, the daily reviewers, and, finally, the vulgar taste of the American people, who refuse to go to the theater except to be entertained, in the crudest sense of that word.

People who care about the theater are likely to care desperately and believe that the failure to produce a great theater is a measure of the total failure of our culture. Because our theatrical critics, despite all their strictures on modern American society, are not usually willing to accept such a pessimistic estimation of our culture, they batter at the theater and attempt to reform it with a violence almost unknown in other kinds of critical writing. New novels may be taken to task, but they are seldom savaged in the manner suggested by the titles of three recent collections of drama criticism: *Curtains, The Acid Test,* and *Seasons of Discontent.* Most of our better dramatic critics seem to be trying to shock our theater to life, to flog it into sanity, to force it to be a true mirror of our times, and thus revitalize society as a whole.

So far these efforts have had little effect upon the theater. So little, in fact, that it is possible to wonder whether anything *can* be done. I am inclined to think that commercialism and Broadway are not the causes of the weakness of our theater but rather the powers that have flowed into and filled the vacuum left by the absence of some unknown quality that provided the impulse for the great theaters of the past.

Though we tend to think of the theater as being as necessary and common a part of a culture as an architectural style or a religion ("If the English had a theater, why shouldn't we?"), the truth is that while every age has some kind of theatrical activity, great Theaters of the kind our critics demand have been extremely rare. In the West there have been only four: in Athens in the last 75 years of the fifth century B.C., in London between 1588 and 1615, in Paris in the middle years of the seventeenth century, and in Europe from about 1880 until shortly after the First World War. Since very few ages have produced a great theater, the question has naturally arisen as to why these ages have while others have not. The usual way of answering the question has been to seek in the historical circumstances of the peoples involved some unique factor that led them to express themselves fully and greatly in the drama. We have been told, for example, that the fifth century Athenians were still close to primitive myth and ritual and therefore naturally expressed themselves and their most basic ideas in pure dramatic terms; or we have been told that the Elizabethans were close enough to medieval Christianity to have a shared sense of life that could be focused and celebrated by all in the theater. I do not doubt that these historical factors contributed something to the greatness of the Greek and Elizabethan theaters, but I find myself for various reasons unable to accept such vast historical generalizations as total explanations of those theaters. It would seem preferable to reverse this historical approach in which the drama is explained by extra-theatrical factors and use the drama itself as a prime historical fact that helps us to say something pertinent about the age and place that produced it. Working from this direction, we would then begin by noting the obvious fact that there are a few widely spaced periods of great drama, and we might then conclude reasonably that these were periods in which men, or at least some of the more interesting and thoughtful men, reasoned and felt in ways peculiarly suited to dramatic expression. We might say, for example, that while lyric poetry flourished in England in the late sixteenth and early seventeenth centuries, that the mind of the age, or at least the most sensitive minds of the age, spoke and thought most effectively and satisfyingly in the dramatic mode. Conversely, we might note that there are numerous ages in which dramatic ways of thinking are not present. For example, each of the great English Romantic poets wanted desperately to be a dramatist, but their plays and the sad condition of the theater in the early nineteenth century reveal that the ways of feeling and understanding at this time were suited not to the dramatic but to the lyric mode.

But what does it mean to "think dramatically"? What is the "nature" of drama, its essential qualities as distinguished from its accidents? Under what "form" does it present life? What is always *done* in every play, no matter what outward shape—killing a king, questioning a god, or blinding oneself—this *doing* takes? As yet we have only begun to phrase these questions, let alone answer them, but perhaps looking at a few of the more obvious facts about the dramatic mode will suggest what it means to "think dramatically." We can note, for example, that men appear in drama as "characters," "actors," or "players of parts," which means that man is presented in the dramatic mode as a creature who plays a role, pretending to be something that he is not—king or salesman—while his reality, if it exists apart from his role, lies beneath his words and costumes and stage titles. Some dramatic characters—Hamlet or Pirandello's Six Characters in search of an author—struggle openly with this necessary condition of their being, trying desperately to strip away the role assigned them and become not a character but truly "themselves." But, of course, there is no escape, as Hamlet discovers, for in the play—and where else can Hamlet exist?—no mode of being is possible except that of character, of player of a role.

But just as the majority of painters and sculptors never understand that to present life in color or in stone is to see it from a definite and exclusive perspective, the majority of playwrights accept the realistic convention that their characters are not "characters" but real people, and so fail to exploit the view of reality implicit in their chosen form. But other dramatists, those who may be said truly to think dramatically, will draw from the inescapable conditions of drama itself the leading ideas of their plays. A self-conscious playwright like Shakespeare, or Pirandello, or Genet will draw attention to the fact that the theater is his chief metaphor for life by frequent use of imagery drawn from playing, by shifting roles, by plays within the play, and by showing his characters trying to create a play. Less self-conscious dramatists who still apprehend the world in dramatic terms will bring form and content into perfect accord by presenting characters who believe themselves to be manifesting their true natures and throwing off the roles imposed by society or the gods, only to discover that they have been playing the assigned role better than they thought: Oedipus, or the revolutionaries in *The Balcony*. Or, a "character" may insist throughout the play that the role in which the world casts him is one that does not properly manifest his truth and seek another role or name which squares with his sense of himself: Willy Loman. Or, in comedy the direction of the play may force a character to accept the role that will bring him happiness, while in tragedy a villain may delight in his marvellous ability to play a variety of roles. Or, a character like Hamlet may come to grips with the essential question posed by the presentation of men as actors and ask whether the dramatic tools—clothes, words, gestures—that man is forced to use can ever manifest that "real" inner self that he apprehends so clearly but that the dramatic view of life cannot present, since each attempt to show it directly becomes another "act."

Infinite variations can and have been worked from the convention of Man-as-Character, and each variation is an exploration of the meaning of the convention itself. The history of drama thus becomes in an unexpected way just that: a history of what it means to understand and cast life in play form.

In our age we are very famiilar with the concept of Man-as-Role-Player, as one who can never entirely know or implement his private sense of self, and in this sense ours is a "dramatic age." But in another sense it is not, for in addition to showing Man-as-Actor in the sense of *pretender,* drama also shows him as actor in the sense of *doer.* While *homo ludens* may never be able to bring inner and outer reality together, he can and must act in drama, and as he acts he begins to make clear his nature by the changes he brings about. "Y'are the deed's creature," says De Flores in *The Changeling* to Beatrice—who persists in believing she is a sweet innocent though she has caused murder—and in these words we hear drama's continuing answer to the problem it poses by showing Man–as–Actor-Pretender. Action is inescapable in drama, and what is done provides the best knowledge possible of men and their world. I can illustrate my point by a brief excursion into the history of the Greek classical theater. By the end of the fifth century B.C., the great tragic dramatists—Aeschylus, Sophocles, and Euripides—had all died, and with them the great drama. At this point, as the drama died, philosophy became the mode in which the Greek world-view was best expressed. There were philosophers before Plato and dramatists after Euripides, of course, and Plato was a very dramatic philosopher while Euripides was a very philosophic dramatist; but at the end of the fifth century the Greek mind began to find philosophy the most congenial mode of expression. Plato's "Analogy of the Cave," which appears in the tenth book of *The Republic,* suggests in part what the shift in modes of statement means. Imagine, says Socrates in that book, a deep cave into which no light penetrates. At the end of the cave sit a group of men, representing the mass of mankind, chained in such a way that they can stare only straight ahead at a wall on which is projected by an apparatus behind them, which they cannot see, a series of silhouettes of natural objects. At some point, by means not specified, one man escapes from the fascination of the images and makes his way out of the cave into the sunlight. Gradually he begins to see such objects as trees and lakes, which he had before known only by their imperfect representations as images on the back wall of the cave. As his sight clears, he begins to lift his eyes and ultimately looks at the sun itself, whose light makes visible all other things in nature. He then makes his way back into the cave, sits down beside the prisoners, and tries to explain to them the difference between the images on the wall and the real objects they imitate. Unwilling to be disturbed in their certainty that what they see is the truth, the prisoners grow very angry with the "philosopher."

This brief parable provides the scheme of most Platonic dialogues, in which Socrates tries to get his audience to realize the gap that exists between their imperfect conceptions of truth and the truth itself. In the end, he so disturbs them that they kill him to silence him and preserve the errors to which they are accustomed and in which they are happy. The crucial point for our purpose, however, is that in this system the philosopher is in possession of a degree of the truth that he has acquired by reason, by contemplation, by inspiration, and by vision. The most characteristic pose of Socrates, the private individual, not the public figure, is standing alone, rapt and utterly oblivious to the material world about him. A man like Alcibiades in *The Symposium* who, while glimpsing the beauties of which Socrates speaks, thirsts so for action that he cannot accept contemplation as a substitute for doing is clearly out of place in the world of the philosopher.

In the drama of the preceding century, however, there is no way of knowing truth without acting and suffering, as Alcibiades does in Sparta and Persia. Each of the great figures of the tragic theater, an Agamemnon, an Oedipus, an Hippolytus, begins with a secure belief that he is by the sheer power of his mind or by the favor of some god in certain possession of the truth, and proceeds to act on this truth. Act he must, for the dramatic form *is* a series of actions or doings. Agamemnon sacrifices his daughter Iphigenia to obtain favorable winds to Troy to punish the rape of Helen by Paris; Oedipus leaves Corinth to outwit the oracle which has foretold that he will kill his father and marry his mother; Hippolytus coolly rejects Phaedra's plea of incestuous love and scorns the demands of Aphrodite. Each action leads inevitably to a reaction, which forces another action, and in the end the train of action leads to events that thought could never have anticipated. "The gods have laid it down," the chorus in the *Oresteia* tells us, that "wisdom comes alone through suffering," and that "dramatic" view of life is borne out by their play, in which the members of the House of Atreus blindly kill and mutilate one another in their search for justice, until at last the sheer horror and number of their crimes makes it possible for them and for the gods themselves to see what they have done, to understand the complexities that turn justice to injustice, and to seek some way out of their agony. The same passage is undergone in *Oedipus the King* and *Oedipus at Colonos,* in which that proud and confident king, who represents all the greatness of mind and pride of Greece, comes at last after the utmost degradation to the sacred grove outside Athens. There, blind and old, he sits with baffling, godlike wisdom before the human figures who move between us and him with their talk of ritual purification, claims of family, the means to earthly power, and the other kinds of wisdom that have not been attained by suffering, by enduring, by being acted upon rather than acting, by being a character in a play written by someone else.

The dramatist and the philosopher do not disagree on the condition of ignorance in which most men live. Plato's image of the
chained figures who stare at the flickering shapes on the cave wall,
taking them for reality, represents perfectly the situation of those
great tragic figures who begin their passages confident that they
know what justice is and that the mind is the measure of all things.
But for the philosopher the way out of this muddlement is through
reason and thought, which step by painful step will lead man away
from his entanglement in our imperfect world toward the realm of
ideas and forms, which nature but imitates crudely.

The dramatic view, on the other hand, says that knowledge can
be acquired only by committing oneself to action and suffering the
consequences. Why this should be is partly a mystery—"the gods
have laid it down"—but it agrees with the familiar views that existence is too complex for man to foreknow the results of his actions,
and that men are so constituted that they often refuse to know anything without the pressure applied by pain. Many of the older
dramatic ways of thinking must have lingered on in Plato, for his
Socrates is a tragic figure who in the end is killed in the darkness of
the cave by those he came to tell of the bright light outside. How
ironic that Socrates should never succeed in bringing any of his
students except Plato—neither great minds like Alcibiades nor the
booby figures who so quickly hold up their hands and parrot, "yes,
how right you are, Socrates"—to any understanding of that ultimate reality he describes so brilliantly.

"Lord, we know what we are, but know not what we may be,"
says Ophelia in her madness, and this view, which is built into the
dramatic form with its requirement of action and development,
brings drama very close to history. History, if taken seriously, is not
a chronicle of the ghastly mistakes and follies of the past—mistakes
and follies that could have been avoided if only the actors had been
as wise and as good as we are—but a record of the continuing
human experiment in which whatever wisdom we have, or choose
to have, was forced out of darkness in the only way possible, by
multitudes of men—who are for the most part nameless—acting in
ignorance and suffering the consequences. The views of drama and
of history are not entirely pessimistic, but they do insist that the
way to knowledge is long, arduous, and infinitely painful.

Henry Ford once said that "History is bunk," and I suppose that
he meant no more than to say that because a thing had not been
done was no reason to think that it could not be done. If you could
cover the world with cheap automobiles by means of new industrial

technology why couldn't you achieve peace, prosperity, and happiness by new methods of social engineering? But Ford's dislike of History implicitly rejects History's painful slowness of change and its refusal to guarantee that change will be for the better.

Ford's view would seem to be the extreme statement of a belief held fairly generally by Americans from the first landings to the present. For all their dourness, the early settlers apparently viewed their new commonwealths as utopias of various kinds, offering escape from the bondage of the past and opportunity to create new societies built from models of the mind rather than developed from traditional institutions. This religious idealism was in time strengthened by the secular idealism of the romantic political theorists who set up the new nation and provided the slogans and banners by which nineteenth and twentieth century America identified itself. The industrial entrepreneurs of the nineteenth century may not seem to have much in common with democrats like Thomas Jefferson, but they did possess a characteristic American scorn for the past noted by Tocqueville and Henry Adams and an optimism about the ability of man to achieve by force of mind and effort of body almost anything he conceived of as desirable. The chief impediments to success were thought to be the outworn attitudes and institutions of the past. Would anyone deny, I wonder, that these attitudes have not only continued to flourish in the twentieth century but have intensified to the point where we as a people believe that what we desire can be achieved instantaneously? "The difficult we do at once, the impossible takes a little longer." Only enough energy and money (and we have plenty of both) need be poured into a project to achieve peace, wealth for all, education, tolerance, slumless cities, and even literature. If we organize well enough, get the right men on the right committees, turn out enough Ph.D.'s, provide enough foreign aid, surely we must be able in a very short period of time to get what we rightly want. As history narrows in on us and we begin to hear voices that say that peace may not come in our time, or that equality of opportunity for all may not come in our generation, we "escalate" our attempts to achieve, now, what must be possible because it is right and good. If we do not, what hope that the changes we desire will ever come about?

Thus with all our efforts, money, and good intentions, we have not yet achieved a theater; and we have not, I believe, because we do not see life in historic and dramatic terms. Even our greatest novelists and poets, sensitive and subtle though they are, do not think dramatically, and should not be asked to, for they express themselves and us in other forms more suited to their visions (and ours). But we have come very close at moments to having great plays, if not a great theatrical tradition. When the Tyrone family stands in its parlor looking at the mad mother holding her wedding dress and knowing that all the good will in the world cannot undo what the past has done to them; when Willy Loman, the salesman, plunges again and again into the past to search for the point where it all went irremediably wrong and cannot find any one fatal turning point; when the Antrobus family, to end on a more cheerful note, drafts stage hands from backstage to take the place of sick actors, gathers its feeble and ever-disappointed hopes, puts its miserable home together again after another in a series of unending disasters stretching from the ice age to the present; then we are very close to accepting our entanglement in the historical process and our status as actors, which may in time produce a true theater.

Most volumes in this series have celebrated and examined the literary triumphs of particular authors and periods. This volume, however, examines not a success but a near-failure. But for those interested in literature and the society it reflects, this can be as interesting as the examination of unquestioned triumph. I have arranged the following articles into broad groups, each of which examines some crucial area of our theater. The individual articles have, in turn, been selected not merely to put the best face possible on our plays and theaters, but to suggest their shared strengths and weaknesses.

Since it is no longer possible in the modern world to consider the drama of one country apart from the drama of the civilization as a whole, I have opened this collection with an article of my own that attempts to discuss the peculiar qualities of the modern theater, of which the modern American theater is very much a part. This is followed by discussions of five of our most successful playwrights. The degree of their success varies considerably, but it is remarkable how similar their plays are in choice of scene and selection of key issues and symbols.

In the next section, "Theaters," I have tried to select articles that will give some idea of the nature and the range of that vast theatrical continuity that reaches from Broadway to some dim, remote area where in the name of theater men and women are busily questioning all of the traditional elements of drama, playscript, plot, character, and acting. Out there, where art gives way to impulse, the theorists still argue with all the subtlety of scholastic philosophers about whether "happenings" are "matrixed" or "non-matrixed," and whether a "happening" is still a "happening" if it is presented twice. Sometimes a note of doubt creeps in: one theorist, after describing a "happening" in which four men in a swimming pool pushed sections of stovepipe back and forth on a red clothesline, points out, rather wistfully, "there was no practical purpose in shoving and twisting the pipes, but it was real activity."

In the section dealing with problems in the theater, I have avoided articles that deal solely with those traditional scapegoats —money, critics, and directors—in favor of three articles that sum up all the usual troubles but go beyond them into an exploration of more basic issues. It seemed only proper to allow the last word to be spoken by a playwright, Edward Albee, who for many represents the best hope for the future of our theater.

The Attempted Dance:
A Discussion of the Modern Theater

by Alvin B. Kernan

A great dramatic tradition impresses itself on the mind not as a series of dates or plot outlines, but as a montage of vivid scenes and arrested gestures, over which human voices hang suspended: asserting, threatening, explaining, questioning. To think of the Elizabethan theater is to see an old man standing on a bare heath in a great thunderstorm shouting at the elements, a young man at night in a walled garden below a balcony looking upward at a beautiful girl, a prince dressed in seafarer's clothing standing in a graveyard holding a skull in his hand. It is to hear such voices as "Thou art the thing itself. Unaccommodated man is no more but such a poor, bare, forked animal as thou art"—"But soft! What light through yonder window breaks? It is the east, and Juliet is the sun!"—"To what base uses we may return, Horatio! Why may not imagination trace the noble dust of Alexander till he find it stopping a bunghole?"

Such scenes as these come to define a theater because each provides a sharply focused image of man in some crucial action. The modern theater also has its great definitive scenes which sum up man as he has come to sense himself in the nineteenth and twentieth centuries—his most fundamental hopes and fears, his understanding of the shape and currents of the world, and his intuition of his stance in relation to that world. At daybreak in a dark Norwegian valley at the head of a gloomy fiord a helpless madman, who has struggled vainly through his life for light and happiness, sees the astronomically distant sun hurling bright light on the snow-cov-

"The Attempted Dance: A Discussion of the Modern Theater" (originally "Introduction") by Alvin B. Kernan. From *Classics of the Modern Theatre*, ed. Alvin B. Kernan (New York: Harcourt, Brace & World, Inc., 1965). © 1965 by Harcourt, Brace & World, Inc. and reprinted with their permission.

ered peaks far above. He speaks flatly to a woman who a moment ago had thought that a decision to face the truth guaranteed happiness: "Mother, give me the sun."

On a bare stage in an empty Italian theater a middle-aged gentleman, who is not a person but a "character," stands trying with great effort to explain the truth of his nature to an uncomprehending director and group of actors whom he *must* persuade to stage his own personal reality in a play. As he speaks, the dreadful truth slowly overwhelms him:

> Each one of us has within him a whole world of things, each man of us his own special world. And how can we ever come to an understanding if I put in the words I utter the sense and value of things as I see them, while you who listen to me must inevitably translate them according to the conception of things each one of you has within himself. We think we understand each other, but we never really do.

A group of Russians sitting by a decayed wayside shrine in a cherry orchard, which had once been their support and justification but is now about to be sold, hear a sound like a breaking harp string, sad and faraway. They speculate aimlessly about whether they have heard the cry of some nameless bird or a lift cable snapping in some distant mineshaft. A moment of silence follows, and then they drift away, each isolated from the others and from a world they no longer understand.

High in the Swedish forests, deep with snow, an old nurse slips a strait jacket on a distraught man, a father, scientist, and one-time army officer, who had thought his authority invincible and his range unlimited, until he entered a death struggle with his wife for control of the family. The man who had once dreamed of a vast world entirely intelligible to the human intellect and manageable by reason sees his dream dissolve into the old, dark nightmare of blind struggle, containment, and death:

> So when we thought the sun should have risen for us, we found ourselves back among the ruins in the full moonlight, just as in the good old times. Our light morning sleep had only been troubled by fantastic dreams—there had been no awakening.

In Central Park, near the zoo, two men quarrel over a bench. Jerry, who speaks for all of the disorders, loneliness, and personal disasters which are censored in the official versions of our affluent society, attempts to force himself on, communicate in some manner

with, Peter, a man who consistently approximates middle-class
statistical norms. It is as if two half-lives, private man and public
man, were coming together for a moment and attempting to join.
But no communication is possible, and in the end Jerry stands impaled on the knife held defensively at arm's length by the frightened Peter.

*   *   *

Such gloomy images and sounds as these dominate the modern
theater, though occasionally scenes of hope and the sound of laughter flash out. Bernard Shaw's supermen, the instruments of the life
force, stand exposing and mocking various kinds of stupidity,
cruelty, and romantic sentimentalism which threaten, but do not
interrupt, the onward movement of life to its unknown goal.
Thornton Wilder's less heroic, comic figures contrive somehow to
escape by the skin of their teeth the traps of an apparently hostile
or indifferent universe and the dangers of their own natures.

Even such a brief collection of scenes as this reveals one peculiar-
ity of the modern theater: its international quality. The other
great theaters of the West were the products of a single language
and a single culture, even though that culture faced a crisis at the
time it produced its great drama—fifth century Athens, the London
of Elizabeth and James I, and the France of Cardinal Richelieu
and Louis XIV. But the modern theater is the product of nearly all
the languages of the Western world, and its settings have ranged
from the isolated country houses of the Russian upper-middle class
to the fiords and forests of Scandinavia, from the arid plains of
Andalusia to a bench in Central Park.

The subject matter of this theater has been as diverse as its languages and settings. Beginning as it does in the mid-nineteenth century, it has embodied at one time or another each of the major
theories about the nature and destiny of man which have emerged
in the last one hundred or so years. The realistic settings and the
natural speech of plays by Ibsen, Chekov, and Hauptmann give
solid form to the general philosophy of naturalism which is,
roughly, the view that man's life is shaped entirely by his social and
physical environment. Brecht's characters, struggling with the demands of earning bread and seeking shelter, constantly engaged in
economic warfare, dramatize the world view of Marx. Relativism,
the view that nothing, neither time nor morals, is absolute, finds
its theatrical voice in the characters of Pirandello who try futilely
to explain to others their personal sense of themselves, while the

others interpret those explanations according to their own particular sense of things. The constant war between men and women, the grotesque sexual antagonisms, of Strindberg's plays give dramatic form to the theory of biological determinism and social Darwinism. Fabian socialism and a tempered belief in progress become the answer to the injustices and confusions of nineteenth century imperialist politics, laissez-faire economics, and Victorian morality in the plays of Shaw. The existentialist belief that man is an absurd creature loose in a universe empty of real meaning finds expression in the plays of Ionesco, Sartre, and Camus. Finally, the psychology of Freud has in the last twenty or thirty years very nearly replaced traditional theories of motivation in such plays as those of Betti, Williams, and O'Neill.

These new ideas have by no means entirely usurped the modern stage, but continue to exist in uneasy mixture or in violent opposition with older, more traditional views of man and nature. While Yeats wrote poetic plays for the Abbey Theater dealing with the ancient Gaelic legends in which ideals triumphed over vulgar reality, Sean O'Casey wrote grimly realistic plays for the same theater dealing with slum life in Dublin during the Irish Rebellion—plays which demonstrated the sham of such ideals as patriotism and duty because they destroyed life rather than fostered it. Similarly, playwrights such as Lorca, Cocteau, and Fry have continued to see in poetry ("poetry of the theater" in Cocteau's case) the power to open up new and unsuspected areas of reality, while Ionesco has devoted himself entirely to showing the emptiness of language because of its inability to communicate even the most simple facts. And while T. S. Eliot has written several verse plays that turn on the miraculous changes wrought in some lives by grace and Christian vision, Samuel Beckett's characters wait, vainly, on a nearly bare stage for some saving power whose name is uncertain and who never appears, who may have come and gone unnoticed, or who may not even exist.

The styles of modern drama are nearly as varied as the settings and the ideas which have informed the plays. A Greek tragic dramatist of the fifth century B.C. wrote in a tradition which prescribed the use of certain poetic meters, limited the number of characters who could appear on stage at one time, made obligatory the provision of odes and dances for a chorus, and directed that the plot must be drawn from heroic legend and the myths of the distant past. Modern dramatists work in no such dramatic tradition, and they have been left entirely free to choose subjects and invent new dramatic styles. The result has been a bewildering number of styles: realism, naturalism, poetic drama, symbolism, expressionism, the epic theater, the theater of the absurd, and surrealism, to name only the most prominent among them. As a result of this freedom, modern plays have taken nearly every possible shape and size, ranging from imitations of Elizabethan tragedy in blank verse to modified Japanese Noh plays; from sprawling plays which take half a day to perform and seek to encompass all of human life (Ibsen's *Emperor and Galilean*, Strindberg's *To Damascus*, O'Neill's *Mourning Becomes Electra*), to brief one-act "anti-plays" which prove the impossibility of finding any meaning in life except its meaninglessness (Ionesco's *The Chairs* or Albee's *The Sand Box*).

What is true of the dramatic form and style of the modern theater is equally true of the acting styles. The dominant mode of acting has been some modification of the Stanislavsky method (developed around the turn of the century at the Moscow Art Theater), which trains an actor, in effect, to lose his own personality while on the stage and become the character he is playing. This is the extension into the player's art of the realistic style, for just as the realistic stage is thought to become not a symbolic representation of reality but an actual place, so the Stanislavsky actor ceases to be a player representing someone else and is transformed into the character. But while this has been the dominant acting style, the reactions against it have been constant and extreme: Brecht trained the actors of his *Berliner Ensemble* to remember always that they were on stage playing a part, and actors at the Abbey Theater in Dublin, it is said, were frequently rehearsed in barrels in order to restrict their movements and to force them to concentrate on speaking their poetic lines, thus reminding them that they were no more than voices for the poetry, necessary but ultimately unimportant instruments of the author.

Attitudes toward stage designs and sets have been similarly various. One end of the range is marked by the meticulously realistic drawing-room sets of Ibsen, where the furniture, rugs, and draperies on the stage were chosen to create the illusion of rooms as real as those the audience had just left in coming to the theater. The general concern for realism led ultimately to such extremes as getting every detail on the costumes, down to the last button, historically accurate for period pieces, and the introduction of water taps that really worked, real doors, genuine gravel for walks, and television sets that showed the same program you would have seen if you hadn't come to the theater. This drive to make the stage a photographic imitation of the actual world remains in many ways the main current of the modern theater, though it has been resisted from the beginning by those who have argued that the stage is by nature a symbolic place, not an illusion of reality, and that settings and costumes should be designed with their symbolic function in mind. This view, most properly termed expressionism, has led to the construction of improbable sets in which skeletal structures represent houses, where the world is reduced to a bare stage with a single tree, where a few folding chairs stand for an automobile and household furnishings. On the expressionistic stage the world may be symbolized by a few angular pieces of abstract statuary, by a color alone, or by a few boards made into platforms of different levels; tall buildings may lean over a house to express menace, stables may flower at their peak to express hope, men may walk through mirrors to express their insubstantiality. The laws of nature and probability are suspended on the expressionistic stage, and their place is taken by the laws of poetry, which state that the writer is free to reshape the natural world in order to make his point clear.

In every area of the modern theater—language, setting, dramatic style, acting technique, theme, stage decor—we seem to find diversity, heterogeneity, and open conflict. Instead of a smoothly developing tradition, a continuing exploitation of a limited number of theatrical resources, and an ever narrowing and finer focus on a few key ethical and metaphysical questions—all the marks of the great theatrical traditions of the past—the theater of the modern age seems to jump nervously and without progression from extreme to extreme, from one bizarre experiment to its opposite, and from one explanation of human nature to its reverse. So great is this diversity that Francis Fergusson has been able to argue most persuasively that what we have is not a true "theater," which focuses "at the center of the life of the community the complementary insights of the whole culture," [1] but only a collection of plays loosely related by the accident of having been written in the same historical period, the late nineteenth and the twentieth centuries. Fergusson explains that this is so because our age lacks any common view of life and man and history:

Human nature seems to us a hopelessly elusive and uncandid entity, and our playwrights (like hunters with camera and flash-bulbs in the depths of the Belgian Congo) are lucky if they can fix it, at rare in-

[1] Francis Fergusson, *The Idea of a Theater* (Princeton, 1949), p. 2.

tervals, in one of its momentary postures, and in a single bright, exclusive angle of vision.[2]

If Fergusson is right, there is no hope of seeing modern drama as a significant whole. The best that can be done is to gather together a group of modern plays and to allow each to present its peculiar view of man and his world. Across one stage let Freudian man move in a painful attempt to exorcise his own and his family's psychic history; on another stage let Marxist man move in the search for the means of production and the socialist utopia; on still another stage let existentialist man move toward that free and irremediable act which will establish his identity. Taken at this level, the views of man which our theater has offered us are difficult if not impossible to reconcile as complementary visions of the same man and the same world. But while the characters who appear on our stage may seem so different, they stand always in the same place, in front of a common background which reflects some shared sense of the human condition. To understand this fact, we must turn to the physical arrangements of our playing houses, and a word of explanation is needed here about the view of the physical theater I am about to offer.

We know that social situations and technological ability affect the architectural style and buildings of a period, but we also know by now that a style, such as the Gothic or the Baroque—embodied in buildings such as Chartres or St. Peter's—is an index to far more than the labor available in a given time and the ability to carve stones or work in plaster. These styles and buildings are, finally, the reflection in stone and space of a people's most fundamental values: their basic sense of themselves and the world they live in. What is true of a cathedral or a palace is likely to be true of a theater, which, at least at some times, has focused man's sense of himself and his world as finely as his churches or his civic buildings. As the drama of a great age tells us as much about that culture as its theology and its laws, so its theaters tell us as much as do its cathedrals and palaces.

Description of the physical theater (the size of the theater, the location of the stage, the costuming, machinery, and sets) has been the province of theater historians. They have tended to give us objective measurements in feet and inches and factual descriptions of the outstanding features of various theaters. Most often they have treated the change in theaters over a period of time and the devel-

[2] *The Idea of a Theater*, p. 1.

opment of new theatrical arrangements as evolutionary processes driven along by social events and technological advances. For example, the large indoor theaters built in the eighteenth and nineteenth centuries might be described as the result of improved engineering skill which allowed builders to span greater spaces without supporting pillars, and of an increase in the wealth and size of the middle class, which resulted in an increase in the number of people who would pay to go to the theater because they had leisure time for culture or because they wished to advertise their new prosperity in public.

As a result of the patient researches of theater historians, however, it has become apparent that each age and culture builds a particular *type* of theater, the external and decorative elements of which it may modify a great deal while leaving the basic form untouched. Consider for a moment the theater of classical Greece, where the plays of Aeschylus, Sophocles, and Euripides were performed. It was an open theater built along an axis. At one end, on seats going up the hillside, the population of the city was seated. Directly in front of them, and partly within the arms formed by the seats, was the circular orchestra or dancing floor, where the chorus of some twelve dancers chanted their odes and moved in intricate but orderly dances. This chorus was bewildered by trouble, usually incapable of direct action, and its members voiced the most conservative opinions about the actions which took place on the low stage directly before them. Here on this stage—we know little about its details—stood the two or three actors, the *doers*. Their costumes made them larger than life size, as befitted the heroes who met and challenged the mysterious powers, the will of Zeus and the other gods, which resided in the great blue sky which arched over the entire theater and formed the permanent backdrop for an Agamemnon, an Oedipus, or a Phaedra. From this mystery came curses on great houses, plagues on great cities, and frightening oracles for great men. But these terrors were met at the stage by great men who acted, suffered, and persevered until at last the mystery was clarified, the weight of ignorance was lifted, and the gods themselves, on some occasions, were forced to materialize on the stage and explain themselves. As the heroes by their pride and pain and loss gradually penetrated the mystery, the chorus behind them absorbed the new knowledge, embodied it in odes, and transmitted it by way of language and dance back to the audience which, always visible, was the human backdrop, the body of society, at the end of the theater opposite the great sky.

To move from the Greek to the modern theater is to move from a vast lighted space organized along a line to a small, isolated area located in the midst of an infinitely extended darkness. At the front of the covered auditorium, elevated above the seats, is a rectangular opening, the proscenium arch, varying in size from theater to theater. The opening in the arch is covered with a curtain while the auditorium is filling and the house lights are on. When the audience has been seated, a switch is thrown, the house lights go out, and the audience has been obliterated. There no longer is a community present, as there was in the Greek and Elizabethan theaters, where the assembled citizens were a passive but very real part of the theatrical symbolism. The curtain rises, the stage lights go on, and before us is our theater: an illuminated box with a few objects in it, floating in a darkness which extends to infinity in every direction. Out of this darkness and into the spotlights come a few actors to speak and struggle for a brief time and then retire, or be carried, back into the darkness out of which they came. The business transacted, the curtain falls and the theater empties.

In the past hundred years this basic theater has been modified in many ways. Projecting platforms have been thrown forward of the arch into the audience, the physical arch has been removed and the entire stage has been made into a circle in the center of the audience, actors have entered and exited through the auditorium in an attempt to extend the stage to the entire theater. Each of these changes has been an attempt to reach the audience, to bring the community back into the theater, but each has failed, and the actor remains isolated in the small area defined for a brief time by the stage lights. The changes do modify the symbolic values of theater in some ways: so long as the actors remain behind the proscenium arch, in that room with the fourth wall removed created by the box set, there are definite boundaries to their situation, their world is small but very solid; once they move onto a platform in the center of the audience with their acting area defined only by spotlights, their space becomes more vague, the surrounding darkness presses closer and menaces the area of light more constantly.

This theater is well known to all of us, so well known that we have lost all sense of its strangeness and ceased to wonder, as with most familiar things, about what it suggests. But here in this arrangement of light, space, and actors is focused a basic sense of the universe and man's position in it which has been shared for some time now by men who otherwise hold violently opposite views. Obviously the existentialist playwright, a Sartre or a Camus, finds himself very much at home in a theater which states by its very arrangements that man with all his "absurd" longings for meaning and validation by some transcendent power is, in fact, isolated in an empty and meaningless universe where he must carve out his own justification and even his own being by a series of acts. But can a religious playwright adjust himself to such a bleak image of time and space? Apparently he cannot if he wishes to show a world in which some certain metaphysical order exists outside man and fills that darkness beyond the narrow confines of the illuminated stage. T. S. Eliot's attempts to dramatize visions and bring spirits into the theater are a history of the awkwardness and frustration inevitable in any attempt to say in our theater what that theater seems designed to deny. But there are religious views, perhaps more common in our times than simple piety, which see the age of miracles as past and regard the life of the spirit as one of constant anxiety and a struggle to maintain a faith which flickers intermittently in a universe which never answers it unequivocally. Religious views of this kind—and by "religion" I mean here all beliefs in some metaphysical power—have found our theater well suited to their sense of the human condition. Robert Bolt in his *Man for All Seasons* and John Osborne in his *Luther* have, for example, recently presented men of powerful religious convictions, Thomas More and Martin Luther, whose sense that they were in touch with and acting in the name of some divine power derived much of its tragic intensity from the great darkness surrounding those stages where they were forced, unsupported, to defy mighty princes and great states. Whatever certainty they found came only from their own hearts. If the same theater and the basic world view it manifests can contain approaches to life as widely separated as existentialism and Christian humanism, it can without difficulty also contain Freudian psychology and conventional morality, explanations of life based on Marxian economic analysis and those based on the meaninglessness of money and possessions, and the host of other rational theories which have been advanced in plays as explanations of and solutions to the basic human condition posited by the form of our theater.

So far we have looked at only the larger dimensions of the modern theater, but we need now to take a closer look at the stage, for if this small illuminated island lost in the vastness of space is our acting ground, what is placed on this stage is of crucial importance. It will represent the substance of the world. We can begin again by a comparison with the Greek and Elizabethan stages. The Greek actor at the Theater of Dionysus in Athens acted, most frequently, in front of a stage house with pillars and portals which represented the palace of the rulers of the city or a temple of its gods. The ground in front of the stage, the dancing floor, thus became the city square, where the frightened chorus, perhaps the elders of the city, assembled to appeal to their rulers, the princes and the gods. In the center of the orchestra was an altar for sacrifices to the gods. Behind the stage house was the sky and the landscape from which the gods might appear at any time, lowered onto the stage by a machine or, less spectacularly, walking on to mingle with the actors. Thus most actions in the Greek theater took place in the context of the principal symbols, the ultimate foundations, of the Athenian world— the social and the heavenly order, the city, the palace, the temple, the abode of the mysterious gods.

Something of the same kind of symbolism was built into the Elizabethan stage. The canopy over the stage was gorgeously painted on the underside to represent the order of the heavenly bodies, a trap in the floor led to an area below the stage known as the cellarage or hell. The areas at the back of the stage was splendidly decorated and could represent, with its upper balconies, the palace of a king or his throne room, the walls of a city or the house of a citizen. One writer has argued that the entire acting area was so constructed that it symbolized simultaneously "a castle, a throne, a city gate, and an altar. It was a symbol of social order and of divine order—of the real ties between man and king, between heaven and earth." [3] If this is so, no matter how much the actions and speeches of the characters might question the meaning and order of life, these solid symbols would stand to remind the audience of the unchanging social and religious order which their theater was built to affirm.

Our theater, however, has no such built-in symbols. At the back of the stage there is only a blank wall or a cyclorama. It is left to our authors and stage designers to fill the space and mark the boundaries of the stage in any way they wish, and they have done this in some very strange ways; indeed one might even say that each of the dramatic styles mentioned earlier—realism, expressionism, symbolism, epic theater, theater of the absurd—has given us a different kind of setting; but in general we can distinguish two major styles, again realism and expressionism, and trace a general trend in our theater from one to the other—though both have existed side by side from the beginning of the modern theater.

[3] George R. Kernodle, "The Open Stage: Elizabethan or Existentialist?" *Shakespeare Survey,* 12 (1959), 3.

Realism, like all other styles, has had its excesses: real forests planted in tubs to provide the actors with living trees to climb, entire houses complete with brick chimneys constructed by carpenters and masons, and—summit of paradox!—gauzy curtains hung over the stage to provide a "realistic illusion" of such places as the forest outside Athens where the elves and fairies dance in *A Midsummer Night's Dream*. But the characteristic set of realism has been more modest and more sensible. It has been most often an interior set, such as that in Ibsen's *Ghosts* or Strindberg's *The Father*, with painted flats to suggest side walls in perspective, doors and windows that open and close, and the type of furnishings which would be found in a room of the same kind outside the theater. When the realistic set tries to reflect the outdoors, it offers, by means of paint and objects, the same sense of familiar reality. If at the edges of the realistic stage we see a most unsettling cosmic and temporal darkness, inside we see a most ordinary and familiar world of tables, chairs, rugs, bushes and trees. And the actors who move within this set increase our sense of familiarity by wearing clothes such as we wear, speaking not in blank verse but in the kind of prose we think we might hear on the street, and revealing motives very like those we expect in ordinary life.

When this realistic set first began to appear in the modern theater, around 1870, it was a great relief from the painted sets of Swiss chalets and far-away castles in Spain which had been (and still are) the staple of the popular romantic drama and opera. The exotic Bulgarian mountains and village in which *Arms and the Man* is set are a spoof of this romantic tradition, and as Shaw's play proceeds it becomes clear that the setting of moonlight and balconies is as unrealistic as are the attitudes toward life held by the figures from musical comedy with whom Shaw peoples his play. Only Bluntschli, the hard-headed Swiss soldier of fortune and hotel-keeper, is out of place in this operatic world. His solid, realistic approach to personal problems, his plain language which cuts through pretense, and his common sense belong, properly, in the new realistic sets where the realism of the stage setting signaled a realistic approach to life and a concern not with romance but with actual social problems. Even today the realistic set is thought to stand for a solid, sensible, down-to-earth treatment of life, and dramatists are praised for their "realism."

No doubt some dramatists do use realistic sets simply as appropriate places in which to locate their plays about the ordinary lives of ordinary people, but the great masters of the realistic style—

Ibsen, Chekov, Strindberg, Shaw—used their sets, which appear to have been assembled at random out of the prop room to imitate day-to-day reality, as symbolic forms, carefully chosen and arranged to define the material world in which the characters must live and through which they must struggle to achieve their ends. Some sense of this can be gained by noting the extreme care with which Ibsen creates and places on his stage such ordinary objects as stoves, pictures, bric-a-brac shelves, and tables. He is not merely constructing a typical Norwegian room in an upper middle-class home of the late nineteenth century—any property-room man could do this. He is arranging his set to symbolize the social and material world in which his characters are so trapped and deadened. Overstuffed chairs which swallow up the character who sits in them, heavy draperies which blot the outside light, furniture which in its very weight and richness denies the existence of the spirit, and in its cluttered placement on the stage constantly interrupts the free movement of the characters who try to stride directly and purposefully through it. The movement of Ibsen's characters has been described as an attempted dance "the opening steps of which are constantly being broken off and replaced by something else" [4] as the character encounters some solid object such as a table, a bookcase, a paper, a photograph album, an armchair, or a stove. This happens constantly in Ibsen's plays, and can be seen to advantage in *Ghosts,* where the heavy, dark rooms of the Alving house are but the most solid manifestation of the social and material facts, the realities, which everywhere impede Mrs. Alving in her "dance" toward truth and the "joy of life." Just as the furniture impedes her free physical movements on stage, so those other more sinister realities—the smoke of Oswald's pipe, his taste for liquor, Engstrand's carelessness with matches, the pressures of society for conformity, and, finally, the inherited syphilis—impede her efforts to be done with the Alving inheritance and the ghosts of old ideas and old crimes. Ibsen was fascinated with the way in which social and material realities, realized by his set, channel and thwart the human spirit with what very nearly amounts to malevolence, and his realistic set is always a representation of the social and material prison in which the free spirit struggles. Chekov, another master of the realistic style, was peculiarly interested in the indifference of the material world to men and their clownish clumsiness in trying to deal with it. *The Cherry Orchard* opens in a realistic Russian room,

[4] Daniel Haakonsen, "Ibsen the Realist," in *Discussions of Henrik Ibsen,* ed. J. W. McFarlane (Boston, 1962), p. 71.

and within the first five minutes of the play two of the characters demonstrate again and again their inability to deal with the simplest facts of reality: one falls asleep over a book and fails to meet a train he had sat up purposely to meet; another enters with a vase of flowers, which he drops, and bumps into a chair—all this in new boots which he can't keep from squeaking. Throughout the play the characters show in a variety of ways their utter helplessness in dealing with the solid facts of life—with the furniture, frost, gravity, time, and death. In the end all that they have valued, all that is focused in the delicate, fragile cherry orchard, goes down before the indifferent processes of nature, just as their shins are broken by indifferent tables and their backsides by indifferent floors.

Once it is understood that the realistic set, and the realistic style in general, has been used to symbolize the solidity of the material and social worlds in which modern man is isolated, the way is clear to understand in still another way the oneness of the modern theater. While realism remains the dominant style, from the time of Ibsen to the present, there have been a great many experiments in other directions, and frequently an author will fluctuate from style to style, as Strindberg did. In general, these experiments rejected realism's basic tenet that the stage should be set to look like the familiar face of the everyday world, that the characters should speak a prose something like that spoken on the streets, and that their motives and actions should be much like those we normally think we see daily. But a large number of playwrights have constructed their plays on the premise that the function of drama, or any other art, is not to hold the mirror up to objective nature, but rather to provide an "image" of the world, to show it as it appears to our imagination rather than to our senses. For example, a realistic playwright who wished to show the inability of human beings to communicate with one another would create a group of characters moving around a conventional drawing room and talking in a normal way; but as they moved toward one another the furniture would get in their way, as they talked their speech would trail away in nervousness or ineptitude, they would be unable to find appropriate words, and they would express incredulity or fail to understand what another said. The result of their failure to communicate directly would be that the unions—love affairs, business agreements, marriages, friendships—which they had hoped to achieve would trail away into nothing, like their words and gestures.

An expressionistic playwright might go to work directly to express the same theme. He might have his characters pour out spates of nonsense, words without meaning, while at the same time they maintained grammatical form and looked as if they understood the nonsense uttered by others and expected their own to be understood. He might fill the stage with empty chairs, as Ionesco does, and have the characters babble on thinking they are talking to real people sitting in them. As a climax Ionesco has a dumb and illiterate orator deliver some "great" message to these same empty chairs. Writing of this latter kind has had many names, but it can most simply be called expressionism, the style in which the artist dispenses with probability in order to express directly his sense of life in images. Poetry is the most familiar form of expressionism, and all expressionistic drama is in some sense an extension of poetry, depending as it does on visual metaphors to establish its meaning. Man ceases to be *like* some strange monster and is actually presented as a rhinoceros or a bug; life ceases to be *like* a wearying circle and is presented as an endless bicycle race in which characters peddle faster and faster to win prizes which are never awarded.

Expressionism existed in the early years of the modern theater with the symbolic plays of Ibsen, the "dream plays" of Strindberg, and the strange subjective plays of Maeterlinck; but since about 1920 it has become much more prominent. Pirandello, Cocteau, O'Neill, and the postwar German expressionists such as Brecht were but the beginnings of a tide that has run ever more strongly down to the plays of Beckett, Albee, Ionesco, Genet, Arrabal, and many others who write for the theater of the absurd. Even the realistic drama has been strongly influenced by expressionism, and the plays of such realists as Shaw, Sartre, Miller, and Williams have been affected. Expressionism has, in fact, been so powerful that many have argued that we have not one theater but two: the theater of realism, which was dominant in the years 1870-1920, and the expressionistic or absurd theater, from about 1920 to the present. The fact that the physical theater with its symbolic arrangement of the world has not changed argues strongly against such a division, but it can be demonstrated in another way that our expressionistic drama is but an intensified, a more openly poetic, form of the realistic drama which preceded and still accompanies it.

Six Characters in Search of an Author is, in my opinion, the pivotal play in the modern theater. It reveals in the starkest terms possible the meaning of the realistic drama of Ibsen, Strindberg, and Chekov which leads into it and the theater of the absurd which leads out of it. The earlier realistic plays depict man as caught in an alien and hostile environment with which he struggles to achieve his peculiarly human aims with only limited success. Pirandello picked up and intensified this theme, but he perceived that the full meaning of this "human condition" could best be dramatized by showing man as trapped in the theater itself. Given the premises stated by the modern theater, that the world which appears within the illuminated box has meaning only in its own terms, that it is not backed up by metaphysical realities existing outside and beyond it, it follows that the lives of men and the events of history have a stage-like or theatrical quality. We are but actors for a brief time on the stage of the world, and our actions and creations endure for only a moment and pass on into history, just as theater sets go to property rooms and plays into anthologies or oblivion. Men are no more than characters in a play, or not even so much, since characters are at least permanently whatever they are, while real men are forever changing. Yet in this world which resembles a theater men struggle desperately to express themselves, to find for themselves a play (or a life) which will reveal their true natures adequately and give their lives a satisfactory shape, as a skillful playwright does his plot. But where the heroes of the earlier realistic drama sought to achieve some such realistic aim as to be rid of the ghosts of old ideas or to save a cherry orchard, Pirandello goes to the root of things and shows his heroes *trying to be in a play.* And where the earlier heroes found their efforts thwarted by reality, by the nature of things represented by the solid, realistic set, Pirandello's heroes find themselves thwarted by the theater of realism. If Epihodov in *The Cherry Orchard* cannot cross a room without bumping into a table, or Mrs. Alving in *Ghosts* finds herself so trammeled by the demands of society that she can act only in certain accepted ways, the characters of Pirandello's play discover that the realistic theater interferes with and finally prohibits any expression of what they conceive to be their full reality, their true nature. For the stepdaughter the presence of a yellow couch in the room where she was nearly seduced is essential, and for the father it is absolutely necessary that he be given time to explain his very complex motives; but the prop room in the theater has only a green couch, and the requirement that the plot continue to move does not allow the father time to explain himself. At every turn the "realism" of the theater denies the "reality" of the characters.

Pirandello has stated in expressionistic terms the same conflict between *realism* and *reality* which Ibsen, Chekov, and Strindberg stated in realistic terms. In so doing, he clarified the meaning of the realistic plays and showed the way to a host of later expression-

istic plays in which reality is presented as some bizarre form of
prison with man at once a heroic and a ludicrous struggler. It may
seem a very long way from a realistic play like *Ghosts* to an expressionistic play like *The Ghost Sonata,* but the strange room in Strindberg's play with its mummy, its death screen, its cook who steals
all the goodness out of the broth, and the ink pot which always
spills is the same place as that room where Mrs. Alving is locked
with her hopelessly insane son. And the flowering hyacinth in the
conservatory is but a visual expression of the same transcendent
hope which drives Mrs. Alving and her son Oswald toward the
light and "joy of life." The difference between the two plays is that
in the expressionistic *Ghost Sonata* the situation is expressed
through a variety of unusual and bizarre stage images which combine to suggest the grotesque and killing restraints society and life
impose on man, while in *Ghosts* the terror of the human condition
is perhaps blurred in one way and heightened in another, by being
presented in the familiar surroundings of the bourgeois parlor
where everything seems so normal and natural.

While each modern set may reflect reality from a particular van-
tage point, they all seem to say that man finds the material universe
they represent to be antagonistic to his transcendent hopes and the
aspirations of his spirit. In other words, where man is sustained and
his social world substantiated by the great symbols of the Greek and
Elizabethan stages, man on the modern stage finds himself hemmed
in and opposed by the symbols of ours. The sense of entrapment in
society and nature which the sets and arrangement of our theater
express is, of course, a focused form of a general sense of entrapment in nature and time which has grown steadily in Western culture in the nineteenth and twentieth centuries. There is no need
to recapitulate the history of thought since the Romantic revolution, but reference to a few of the leading ideas will serve to make
the point that our theater stands as close to the center of our culture as the Greek and Elizabethan theaters apparently did to theirs.

Once a faith in a supernatural order weakened under the pressure of scientific rationalism, and the belief in an established hier-
archical society began to break up under the attack of democratic
revolutions and the doctrine of absolute equality, individual man
was freed to face nature, society, and himself, and to make them
into what he wanted them to be. Or so it seemed. Yet each great
discovery of the free, inquiring mind, while it promised control
over the accidents of nature and history, turned out, paradoxically,
to show more clearly the isolation of man in time and nature. Dar-

win's great statement on the origin, differentiation, and evolution of the species cut man adrift from his metaphysical origins and placed him in a world where survival belongs to the strong, the ruthless, and the biologically lucky; not to the moral and the just. Marx's investigations of society revealed economic man, the producer and the buyer of goods and services, who bands together with other men only for his own economic advantage and who is willy-nilly caught in a historical movement which pits the have-nots against the haves. Freud's explorations of the mind seemed to extend nature's tyranny over man inward, making him the very nearly helpless victim of unconscious drives and libidinal forces, an automaton dancing to a tune called by internal forces, or a compulsive neurotic twisting into strange shapes in the attempt to repress powers he is not even aware of repressing. Physical science broke up the familiar face of creative nature, with its traditional intimations of some regenerative force, into electrical quantities which can only be measured mathematically. The last familiar markers disappeared when the theory of relativity told us that speed and direction existed only in relation to where we stood.

All these discoveries can be viewed optimistically, of course, and were so viewed by their discoverers, as demonstrations of the power of the human mind to uncover the truth of things and thus lay the grounds for some understanding of the world and life. To believe in this way is to believe in Progress. But it is possible to believe in the necessity of knowing these hard facts and at the same time to recognize that each of them is frightening because it imprisons us in a nature which limits and denies those essential qualities which we feel to be uniquely human: in theological terms, our souls; in humanistic terms, our true natures as men. If we are no more than strugglers for survival adapting to a constantly changing environment; exploiters or exploited caught up in a predetermined class struggle for control of the means of production; walking instruments of inescapable psychological forces, chemical reactions, and social conditioning; if we are all these in a universe we cannot even see truly, where there are no absolute directions or movements, how are we to validate our consciousness, our suffering, our sense of dignity, our demand that life have meaning, our ability to look at all the forces which control us and still withdraw into some area peculiarly ourselves?

For some, these last are simply illusions, fostered by outmoded ways of thinking. For them, the sooner man accepts himself as an object moved about by an interaction of forces and natural laws, the better. But our dramatists have never shared this view. The modern theater has not denied the existence of the deterministic and morally irresponsible universe; rather it has accepted it and embodied it in the construction of its stage, in its sets, and in its plays, where the standard plot shows the entrapment of man in history, society, economics, psychology, and in some form of environment. A history of the modern drama could be written using scenes of entrapment ranging from Old Firs locked in the dying house of *The Cherry Orchard,* or the captain in *The Father* sitting still while his old nurse slips the strait jacket on him, to Mother Courage harnessed to her wagon and Blanche du Bois in *Streetcar Named Desire* trying desperately to call an unknown number for help, while Stanley Kowalski stands grinning in his red pajamas, blocking the door. But two scenes will make the point.

The first is the concluding scene of *Ghosts.* Throughout the play Mrs. Alving and her son Oswald have struggled to free themselves from the gray, dim world forced on them by society, nature, and heredity. Using the play's chief symbols, we could say they have struggled to escape from the darkness into the truth of light. But they thought, like the great rebels and formulators of truth in the nineteenth century, that light and truth would bring "joy of life." When Mrs. Alving rejects the demands of society that unpleasant truths be hidden under a cover of well-seeming, and tells her son that his sickness and the drunken debauchery of his father were the results of heredity and an unfavorable environment, not of moral failing, she breaks into the world of truth. But the truth proves unendurable. Oswald, who is in the last stages of syphilis, goes insane before her eyes, his fear unassuaged and his madness no less terrible for being not his own fault. The son and mother stand at last in the full light of truth, and as the sun rises, shining on the icy peaks far above the dark valley in which they live, the insane son's cry, "Mother, give me the sun," distills modern man's sense of isolation and helplessness in the midst of alien nature. Clarity of vision reveals only the desperateness of the situation in which we long like children for light and heat which originate ninety million miles away to send only the dimmest emanations into our homes.

The other scene is from Lorca's *Blood Wedding,* in which the violent, uncontrollable power of blood and passion, represented by the horse, has destroyed an entire family and wasted a country. Her husband and son dead, a mother sits wondering how it can be that

so small a thing as a knife, a mere piece of steel, can destroy so
great a thing as a man:

> Neighbors: with a knife,
> with a little knife,
> on their appointed day, between two and three,
> these two men killed each other for love.
> With a knife,
> with a tiny knife
> that barely fits the hand,
> but that slides in clear
> through the astonished flesh
> and stops at the place
> where trembles, enmeshed,
> the dark root of a scream.

There is no question in our theater that life is subject to objects so
small as a knife in such strange places as "between two and three,"
but the peasant mother's astonishment that this is so is an astonishment that has kept our theater alive.

When William Butler Yeats first saw a performance of *Ghosts,*
he remarked:

> All the characters seemed to be less than life-size; the stage, though
> it was but the little Royalty stage, seemed larger than I had ever
> seen it. Little whimpering puppets moved here and there in the mid-
> dle of that great abyss. Why did they not speak with louder voices or
> move with freer gestures? What was it that weighed upon their souls
> perpetually? Certainly they were all in prison, and yet there was no
> prison.[5]

Yeats is being disingenuous here, for he knew the prison very well
—his poetry is a record of a heroic struggle with it—and he knew
that it is as real as the stage says it is. But he was right in one way
about the figures in this prison: they are small and ineffective. It is
a commonplace of criticism that our dramatic heroes are but shadows of those of previous days. The figures of Greek tragedy were
demigods, titans, founders of kingdoms, and rulers of great cities.
When they, or the kings and queens of Elizabethan drama, rose or
fell, kingdoms rose or fell with them, and all mankind shared in
their fortunes. But the heroes of modern tragedy are neither so

---

[5] W. B. Yeats, "The Irish Dramatic Movement," in *Plays and Controversies*
(New York, 1924), p. 122.

great nor so powerful in the scheme of things. They are likely to be a group of ineffective, middle-class Russians in some isolated country house, a salesman who tries to sell himself in a territory where no one wants to buy, two tramps waiting on a bare stage, an old woman trying to pull a battered wagon about, or two old people who think they have something of importance to say to the world but don't really know what it is they have to say. Where the fate of kingdoms turned on the actions of earlier heroes, much less is involved in the actions of our heroes: they try to save a cherry orchard, pay for a house and raise their children, wait for someone who will probably never come, or just find someone who will be kind to them.

As their statures and their aims are diminished, so are their voices. Playwrights are frequently exhorted by modern critics to give their characters poetry, and some of our dramatists have tried, without much success. A type of realistic prose, a heightened version of the speech of everyday life, seems to be the most congenial form of speech for our heroes. One of the principal themes of modern drama has been the inability of language to convey the full meanings desired by the speakers, and this theme has been carried in large part by the characters' struggle with the flat, realistic prose they most ofen speak. I am not arguing that Ibsen or Chekov could have written poetry of a quality equal to Shakespeare's had they wished to do so; rather I am suggesting that these and other dramatists of our theater were led away from attempting dramatic poetry of the older variety by the nature of their theme, the isolation of man in a universe where all his environment, including the very language he speaks, thwarts his efforts to express what he feels to be his essential self. Behind the mumbling, inarticulate dying voices of Chekov's characters there are hints of passion and depth of feeling something like Romeo's or Hamlet's, but these feelings are first qualified and lose their force in the mind and are then finally dissipated in the awkward, flat phrases which are the only language available to modern man. The failure of language to express the fullness of self which is implicit in the realistic drama becomes explicit in the expressionistic drama— *The Chairs, Zoo Story*—where we are shown characters who cannot convey any sense of their own reality by words, who babble on in long speeches which sound very serious but mean nothing, who spout open nonsense, or who stand mutely on stage.

But with all the limitations which are imposed on him on the modern stage, man has not given up the struggle on that stage and accepted the role of a machine moved in a predictable manner by a variety of unchanging forces, which his world tries to force on him. No matter how close the darkness may creep toward him—and it has come very close in the most recent plays—he continues to occupy a place in the center of the stage and at least one light still shines on him. His desires remain spacious. Unsupported by any visible metaphysical order, thwarted by society, at odds with external nature and his own being, he still continues to act and to try to tear from the world those things without which he feels he cannot live as a human being: his freedom, his dignity, his reality. In this persistent effort he becomes one with the great strugglers of the older drama who moved toward these same goals, but his chances of success are greatly diminished. Not only is his environment more hostile, but the fact that he is a salesman or a tattered tramp, whose voice no longer fills the theater and batters at the world which denies him, suggests that his chances of success are far less than those of older heroes, and that his success or failure will not disturb the order of things greatly.

Our theater does not underestimate the dangers of the universe in which man lives, but it has not lost faith in man either. When pressed to the extremes, in the bleak place where almost everything has lost its meaning, man on the modern stage at least still waits:

> What are we doing here, *that* is the question. And we are blessed in this, that we happen to know the answer. Yes, in this immense confusion one thing alone is clear. We are waiting for Godot to come—

This waiting is as likely to be the height of foolishness as the absolute of virtue: an ambiguity which haunts most actions on the modern stage. But man, no matter how tattered and inarticulate, is still *there;* he has not yet walked off and left the stage to darkness.

American Blues:
The Plays of Arthur Miller
and Tennessee Williams

by Kenneth Tynan

"Since 1920," Arthur Miller has said, "American drama has been a steady, year-by-year documentation of the frustration of man," and the record supports him. Between the wars most of the serious American playwrights—Odets, for instance, Elmer Rice, Maxwell Anderson, Irwin Shaw, and Lillian Hellman—did their best work in the conviction that modern civilization was committing repeated acts of criminal injustice against the individual. Their heroes were victims, such as Mio in *Winterset,* and they devoted themselves to dramatizing the protests of minorities; it was thus that they ploughed the land cleared for them by O'Neill, the solitary pioneer bulldozer. For his long-sightedness they substituted an absorption in immediate reality; where he was the admonitory lighthouse, they were the prying torches. During the war their batteries ran out: since 1945 none of them has written a first-rate play. The mission of martyrology has been taken up by the younger generation, by Arthur Miller and Tennessee Williams.

Miller and Williams seem, on the face of things, to have even less in common than Ibsen and Bjørnson. Miller, a man of action, belongs to the thirties' tradition of social drama, while Williams, a poet *manqué,* looks ahead to a lyrical, balletic *Gesamtkunstwerk* in which (though I doubt whether he fully recognizes the fact) words as such are likely to have less and less importance. Yet the two men share much. Both echo Jacob in *Awake and Sing,* who

"American Blues: The Plays of Arthur Miller and Tennessee Williams" by Kenneth Tynan. From *Curtains* (London: Longmans, Green & Co. Ltd., New York: Atheneum Publishers, 1961). Copyright © 1961 by Kenneth Tynan. Reprinted by permission of the publishers.

says: "We don't want life printed on dollar bills." Miller is a rebel against, Williams a refugee from the familiar ogre of commercialism, the killer of values and the leveller of men. "You know, *knowledge—ZZZZpp! Money—zzzpp!* POWER! Wham! That's the cycle democracy is built on!" exults the Gentleman Caller in *The Glass Menagerie*. But this is not their only joint exploit. Both reserve their most impassioned utterance for one subject, into which they plunge headlong, sometimes floundering in self-pity, sometimes belly-diving into rhetoric, but often knifing straight and deep: the subject of frustration. Lady Mulligan, in Williams' latest play *Camino Real*, complains to Gutman, the proprietor of her hotel, that he has chosen to shelter some highly undesirable guests. Whereupon:

> *Gutman.* They pay the price of admission the same as you.
> *Lady M.* What price is that?
> *Gutman.* Desperation!

Techniques change, but grand themes do not. Whether in a murder trial, a bullfight, a farce like *Charley's Aunt*, or a tragedy like *Lear*, the behavior of a human being at the end of his tether is the common denominator of all drama. When a man (or woman) arrives at self-knowledge through desperation, he (or she) has become the raw material for a great play. The stature of the work will depend on the dramatist's honesty and skill, but its cornerstone is already laid. Though they take the same theme, Miller and Williams build very differently. In European terms, Miller is the Scandinavian: he has in fact translated Ibsen, whose fierce lucidity, humorlessness, and "odor of spiritual paraffin" he shares. Williams, on the other hand, is the Mediterranean, the lover of Lorca and D. H. Lawrence, sensuous, funny, verbally luxuriant, prone to immersion in romantic tragedy. Miller's plays are hard, "patrist," athletic, concerned mostly with men. Williams' are soft, "matrist," sickly, concerned mostly with women. What links them is their love for the bruised individual soul and its life of "quiet desperation." It takes courage, in a sophisticated age, to keep faith with this kind of love, and their refusal to compromise has led both Miller and Williams into some embarrassing pseudo-simplicities. Their reward is in characters like Joe Keller of *All My Sons*, Willy Loman of *Death of a Salesman*, John Proctor of *The Crucible*, Blanche DuBois of *A Streetcar Named Desire*, Laura of *The Glass Menagerie*, Kilroy of *Camino Real*, who live together in the great theatrical line of flawed, victimized innocents.

Arthur Miller, who was born in Brooklyn in 1915, achieved his first Broadway production at the age of twenty-nine. The play, *The Man Who Had All the Luck,* had a framework which Miller (himself a second son) later elaborated in *All My Sons* and *Death of a Salesman*: the relationship of two sons with their father. The protagonist is David, the elder, an unskilled garage hand in a midwestern town. His brother, Amos, forcibly trained by Pat, a jealous and protective father, to become a baseball pitcher, gets nowhere, while the ignored David thrives, financially as well as maritally. His inability to fail makes David neurotic, and to deaden his sense of unworthiness he falls into the habit of ascribing his success to luck. In the final scene he is made to understand that "luck" is merely a word used by men less diligent than himself to explain his triumphs. "You made it all yourself," cries his wife. "It was always you." His hired man, the immigrant Gus, puts the play's case: a man must believe, he says, "that on this earth he is the boss of his life, not the leafs in the teacup, not the stars. In Europe I seen already millions of Davids walking around, millions. They gave up already to know that they are the boss. They gave up to know that they deserve this world." The point of the *drame à thèse* is weakened because the principal characters are too obviously pawns in Miller's hands; what stays in the mind is the craggy candor of the dialogue. Miller, like Williams, is committed to prose drama, in which both men have uncovered riches which make the English "poetic revival" seem hollow, retrogressive, and—to use Cyril Connolly's coinage—praeteritist.

Pat, David's father, is guilty only by implication. Joe Keller in *All My Sons,* staged by Elia Kazan in 1947, is a criminal in the legal sense. Shadily, he has been acquitted of manufacturing faulty aircraft parts during the war, and when the play opens, his partner is in jail, taking the rap for him. Of Joe's two sons, one has been killed in action, and the other, Chris, intends to marry his brother's ex-fiancée, the convicted partner's daughter. Chris is a militant idealist ashamed of having survived the war; material possessions sicken him unless they have been purely and honorably acquired— "Otherwise what you have is loot, and there's blood on it." Miller concentrates on two shifting relationships: between Chris and his girl, and between Chris and his father. Joe Keller (like Willy Loman) had to compromise in order to live; and Chris (like Biff in the later play) is overwhelmed by the revelation of paternal guilt. How can he marry the daughter of a man who was imprisoned because of his father's perjury? Miller solves this classic impasse with a smart stroke of melodrama: unconvincingly, Keller accepts the burden and shoots himself.

"I'm his father," says Keller at one point, "and he's my son, and if there's something bigger than that I'll put a bullet in my head." This message, more symphonically orchestrated, reappears in Miller's best play, *Death of a Salesman*, which Kazan directed in 1948. *All Our Fathers*, as Daniel Schneider suggested, would be an appropriate alternative title. Willy Loman and his two sons, the sensualist Happy and the mysteriously retarded Biff, are ruined by their belief in "the wrong dream," the mystique of salesmanship. "What are you building?" says Ben, Willy's millionaire brother. "Lay your hand on it. Where is it?" Unlike most hero-victims, Willy is not cynical about the values which are corrupting him; he is pathetic because, brightly and unquestioningly, he reveres them. As the play begins, Biff, the quondam college hero, has returned penniless to his Brooklyn home, where he finds his father going crazy with failure to sell. The ensuing action covers the next twenty-four hours: in a series of beautifully welded interlocking flashbacks we pursue Willy's thoughts into the past, back to the germinal moment of calamity when he was surprised by Biff in a hotel room with a half-dressed tart. This encounter, with its implied destruction of the father-god, stunted Biff's career and left Willy with a load of remorse redoubled by the fact that he, too, was the unsuccessful one of two brothers. Memory explodes the cocoon of illusions within which he preserves his self-respect, and (ostensibly for the insurance money) he commits suicide.

The play is Miller's triumph in the plain style; it rings with phrases which have entered into the contemporary subconscious. "He's liked, but he's not—well liked"; "The woods are burning, boys"; Ben's complacent "The jungle is dark but full of diamonds, Willy." More memorably, there is Mrs. Loman's anguished rebuke to her sons for having scorned their father:

> Willy Loman never made a lot of money. His name was never in the papers. He's not the finest character that ever lived. But he's a human being, and a terrible thing is happening to him. So attention must be paid. He's not to be allowed to fall into his grave like a dog. Attention, attention must be finally paid to such a person.

Charley, Willy's neighbor, speaks an epitaph over him which has the same groping, half-articulate power:

And for a salesman, there is no rock bottom to the life. He don't put
a bolt to a nut, he don't tell you the law, or give you medicine. . . .
Nobody dast blame this man. A salesman is got to dream, boy. It
comes with the territory.

There is a fair amount of otiose breast-beating in the script, and
Miller's prose sometimes slips into a sentimental rhythm of despair
which could be convicted of glibness. But the theater is an impure
craft, and *Death of a Salesman* organizes its impurities with an
emotional effect unrivalled in postwar drama.

Willy Loman goes to his fate without knowing exactly why it has
overtaken him. The heroes of Miller's [next] two plays are also de-
feated, but they know what forces have beaten them: the enemy in
each case is identified. In 1950 he adapted *An Enemy of the People*,
turning it into a racy contemporary pamphlet. His temperament
chimed with what he describes as Ibsen's "terrible wrath," and the
dilemma of Stockmann, the betrayed crusader, duplicated Miller's
own, that of the life-long democrat who learns, from the example
of his own country, that majority rule is not infallible. Stockmann
is vanquished by the pusillanimous stupidity of the mob, on which,
in the original, he launches a furious attack. Miller softens it in
translation, thereby forfeiting the objectivity which allowed even
Ibsen's heroes their weaknesses. Anger is a great simplifier, and
Miller is an angry writer. *An Enemy of the People* marks his decision to weight the scales in favor of the oppressed minority man.
"Before many can know something, *one* must know it"—Stockmann's affirmation steers us towards *The Crucible*, . . . produced
in New York [in January, 1953]. The bird's-eye compassion of *Salesman* has now been replaced by a worm's-eye sympathy which extends only to the "right-minded" characters. Though its draws plain
contemporary parallels with its subject, the witch-hunt at Salem, it
is not an overtly political play: it deals with the refusal of a stubborn intellect to enter into forced allegiances. "I like not the smell
of this 'authority,'" says Proctor, the hero. In Salem, as in Stockmann's township, nonconformity was allied with sin, an attitude
which Miller detests so savagely that the play often resembles the
trial scene from *Saint Joan* with the Inquisitor's speech deleted.
The inquisitors in *The Crucible* are unmotivated fiends, and the
atmosphere in which they flourished is never explored or accounted
for.

The action stays close to historical fact. A group of flighty wan-
tons, charged with engaging in mildly orgiastic rites in a wood near

Salem, hit on the notion of exculpating themselves by accusing their neighbors of having sent the devil into them. Their accusations are believed; a tribunal is set up; and the hangings begin. Proctor's wife is arrested, and his attempts to exonerate her lead to his own arrest. In a fine, clinching line he demands: "Is the accuser always holy now?" If he confesses, giving a list of those who infected him with diabolism, he will be freed; if not, he will be executed. At their last meeting his wife tells him how another of the condemned died:

> Great stones they lay upon his chest until he plead aye or nay. They say he give them but two words. "More weight," he says. And died.

Head high, as the drums roll, Proctor sacrifices himself for his principles, a commonplace "Victorian" martyrdom worthy of a mind much less subtle than Miller's. *The Crucible* is disturbing because it suggests a sensibility blunted by the insistence of an outraged conscience: it has the over-simplification of poster art.

In *The Devils of Loudun,* a much more searching analysis of witch-hunting, Aldous Huxley mentions the euphoria of the "adrenalin addict," a type to which Miller seems at present to belong. "There are many people," Huxley says, "for whom hate and rage pay a higher dividend of immediate satisfaction than love," this satisfaction being derived from "their psychically stimulated endocrines." Bad temper, which produces cramp in the creative muscles, is an enemy of art; and though *The Crucible* is on the right side morally, socially, and politically, it is the artistic equivalent of a closed shop. Full of affirmations, it is also full of emotional half-truths; which will do for a leader-writer, but not for a playwright of Miller's giant stature.

Tennessee Williams' genius has no social commitments, but many aesthetic ones. His faults, like Miller's, are the defects of his virtues. The present cast of Miller's mind traps him in the present, the male preserve wherein history is shaped, and the universal preoccupation is with action and incident; Williams trades in nostalgia and hope, the past and the future, obsessions which we associate most strongly with the great female characters—Marguérite Gautier, Cleopatra, Hedda Gabler, and Chekhov's women, none of whom cares for today half as much as she cares for yesterday or tomorrow. His plays thus have the static quality of dream rather than the dynamic quality of fact; they bring the drama of mood to what may be its final hothouse flowering.

Williams is a Southerner, born [in 1911] in Columbus, Missis-
sippi, and his work first reached Broadway when his "memory
play," *The Glass Menagerie,* was produced in 1945. It turns a burn-
ing-glass on to a storm-proof family unit, insulated against life by
its careful preservation of gentility. A stage direction reads:

> The apartment faces an alley, and is entered by a fire-escape, a
> structure whose name is a touch of accidental poetry, for all of these
> huge buildings are always burning with the slow and implacable fires
> of human desperation.

Here live Amanda, garrulous and suffocatingly maternal, her
cynical son, Tom, and her crippled daughter, Laura. Retrospec-
tively, Tom tells the story of how he invited a Gentleman Caller
to dinner as a possible beau for Laura, and how the Caller, affable
though he was, revealed that he was already spoken for. Laura's
spinsterhood is confirmed; Amanda's hopes are dashed; but neither
of these minor disasters is made to sound mawkish. Williams' wry
wit acts as a caustic to the wounds. In Amanda, fussy and conversa-
tionally archaic, he shows the perfection of his ear for human
speech, and also the extent of his tact: she never becomes a grotesque. The play is not a major achievement, but its opacity is as
precise and marvellous as a spider's web.

You Touched Me!, on which Williams collaborated with Donald
Windham, is of interest only because it dealt (like *The Glass Menagerie*) with the impact of reality on illusions, in this case on two
isolated, mutually infectious virgins; and because it was adapted
from the short story of the same name by D. H. Lawrence, one of
Williams' heroes. It was followed in 1947 by *A Streetcar Named
Desire,* which was directed by Kazan, who seems to have an instinct
for the best of both Miller and Williams. It is perhaps the most
misunderstood of his plays: the English and French productions
were both so blatantly sensationalized that Williams' underlying
lyric fiber passed unnoticed. If Willy Loman is the desperate average man, Blanche DuBois is the desperate exceptional woman.
Willy's collapse began when his son walked into a hotel apartment
and found him with a whore; Blanche's when she entered "a room
that I thought was empty" and found her young husband embracing an older man. In each instance the play builds up to a climax
involving guilt and concomitant disgust. Blanche, nervously boast-
ful, lives in the leisured past; her defense against actuality is a sort
of aristocratic *Bovarysme,* at which her brutish brother-in-law Stanley repeatedly sneers. Characteristically, Williams keeps his detach-

ment and does not take sides: he never denies that Stanley's wife, in spite of her sexual enslavement, is happy and well-adjusted, nor does he exaggerate the cruelty with which Stanley reveals to Blanche's new suitor the secrets of her nymphomaniac past. The play's weakness lies in the fact that the leading role lends itself to grandiose overplaying by unintelligent actresses, who forget that when Blanche complains to her sister about Stanley's animalism, she is expressing, however faintly, an ideal:

> Such things are art—as poetry and music—such kinds of new light have come into the world since then! . . . That we have to make *grow!* And *cling* to, and hold as our flag! In this dark march toward whatever it is we're approaching . . . *Don't—don't* hang back with the brutes!

When, finally, she is removed to the mental home, we should feel that a part of civilization is going with her. Where ancient drama teaches us to reach nobility by contemplation of what is noble, modern American drama conjures us to contemplate what might have been noble, but is now humiliated, ignoble in the sight of all but the compassionate.

In 1948 Williams reworked an earlier play, *Summer and Smoke.* Its heroine, Alma, is Blanche ten years younger: a Southern virgin concealing beneath "literary" affectations a sense of inadequacy in the presence of men. Her next-door neighbor, a notorious rake, tries to seduce her and is boldly repulsed. He shows her an anatomy chart, and explains that the human body is a tree inhabited by three birds, the brain, the belly, and the genitals. Where, he asks, is the soul of which she speaks and for which, in Spanish, her name stands? Ironically, he ends up reformed, whereas Alma, her sexual instincts newly awakened, moves to the other extreme. They exchange attitudes, passing almost without contact. *Summer and Smoke,* a needlessly symbolic morality play, is sentimental in that its characters are too slight to sustain the consuming emotions which are bestowed on them.

Nobody could say that *The Rose Tattoo* (1950) did not contain large characters. It is the most thoroughgoing star vehicle of the last ten years, expressly written for Anna Magnani, whose shaky acquaintance with English unfortunately prevented her from playing the lead in the stage production. Here Williams pleads the cause of sexual love as its own justification. "So successfully," he says in his preface, "have we disguised from ourselves the intensity of our own feelings, the sensibility of our own hearts, that plays in the tragic tradition have begun to seem untrue." At a time when Miller's plays were growing colder and more intellectualized, Williams' blazed hotter and more sensuous. His heroine is a poor Sicilian immigrant whose husband, a truck-driving smuggler with a fabulous capacity for sexual devotion, has been shot. She learns to her horror that her man had been faithless to her, but the realization does not prevent her from joyously taking as her new lover a man who physically resembles the dead ideal. The play's complex structure— short scenes linked by evocative snatches of music—is too poetic for its theme, but the virtuosity of the writing, alternately ribald and pathetic, is tremendous. Does it alternate between tragedy and farce? That is because it was meant for a great actress whose gift it is to switch emotional gear, change from a Siddonsesque pose to a bout of nose-picking without a moment's hesitation. Williams' fault, as in *Streetcar,* was to have overestimated English-speaking actresses. It would take a Magnani to play the scene in which Serafina, the heroine, entertains her new lover, out of whose pocket, as the poetic tension mounts, there falls a neatly packaged contraceptive. Sardou never asked as much of Bernhardt, nor D'Annunzio of Duse.

Kazan renewed his association with Williams in the spring of 1953, when he directed the violently controversial *Camino Real.* This is a phantasmagoria of decadence, as limpidly rebellious to modern civilization as a Bix Beiderbecke solo is to a Paul Whiteman orchestration. The published text has a unity never achieved by the acting script. It carries to its conclusion Williams' dictum: "I say that symbols are nothing but the natural speech of drama." In a preface he adds: "I have read the works of 'thinking playwrights,' as distingushed from us who are permitted only to feel. . . ." The result is a tranced play of hypersensitivity, a weird drug-work of wit, terror, and inertia.

It is set in a mythical Central American coastal town. Stage left is the Seven Seas Hotel, where live Byron, Casanova, and Marguérite Gautier, ghosts of the aristocratic way of life; stage right are a pawnbroker's shop, a fortune-teller's tent, and a flophouse, where, among the outcasts, we encounter the Baron de Charlus. Upstage is an arch, giving on to a desert, where a hot wind blows and whither no one dares travel. Williams' hero is Kilroy, the new arrival at this fetid microcosm of modern life: the embodiment of youth and enterprise, he was once a prizefighter but had to abandon his career because "I've got a heart in my chest as big as the head of a baby." He is elected the town butt, and the police deck

him out in a clown's costume, complete with electrically sparking
nose. How does this simpleton fit in with the filth of the Camino
Real? Williams answers the question in writing which seems too
often to have been composed in a state of *kif*. He indulges in vague,
roseate aphorisms; nor can he resist theatrical shortcuts such as a
noisy airplane crash and *two* chases down the aisles and into the
boxes of the theater, devices which assist the play about as tellingly
as a consignment of heroin would help an anti-narcotics campaign.
Yet out of the strident blare of the action, Williams' faith in Kilroy's truth, in a child's mistrust of phonyness, emerges with overwhelming clarity. For those anarchists who escape he has undis-
guised sympathy. Byron, for example, says of his later works: "They
seem to improve as the wine in the bottle—dwindles. . . . *There
is a passion for declivity in this world*"; but when, having roused
himself, he departs into the murderous desert, Williams gives him
a splendid epitaph: "*Make voyages!—Attempt them!*—there's nothing else!"

Kilroy, too, attempts the voyage, but only after a serio-comic encounter with a character called the Gypsy, who organizes and ad-
vertises the local fiesta, at which her daughter, in a loony parody of
a fertility ritual, annually recovers her virginity. The Gypsy's gar-
ish cynicism ("File this crap under crap") struck the New York
critics as the most recognizable thing in the play, along with Kilroy's seduction of the Gypsy's daughter, a grossly comic scene in
which the two young people repeat to each other eight times the
talismanic words: "I am sincere." Surviving a brisk attempt to
murder him, Kilroy journeys through the perilous arch, accompanied by Don Quixote, that other liegeman of the lost cause, who
ends the play with a movingly symbolic cry: "The violets in the
mountains have broken the rocks!"

Many charges can be brought against *Camino Real*. It has too
many italics, too many exclamation marks; it depends too much on
boozed writing and aureate diction. Its virtue is in its affectionate
championing of the flyblown, inarticulate stratum of humanity.
Perhaps when Quixote and Kilroy reach the snowy upper air of the
unnamed mountains, they will become subjects for a play by Miller,
whose artistic life is dedicated, like Shaw's, to a belief in progress
towards an attainable summit. William's aspirations are imaginative and hence unattainable; and therein lies the difference between
them.

Complementary, yet irreconcilable, Miller and Williams have
produced the most powerful body of dramatic prose in modern

English. They write with equal virtuosity, Williams about the violets, Miller about the rocks. The vegetable reinforces the mineral; and the animal, a dramatic element feared or ignored in the English theater, triumphantly reinforces both.

The World of Thornton Wilder

by Tyrone Guthrie

My first encounter with Thornton Wilder as a man of the theater was in Glasgow about 1930. I was judging a competition between amateur dramatic societies; a Jewish group offered what I recall as a brilliant performance of *The Long Christmas Dinner*. This short play fascinated me because it discarded a lot of theatrical conventions of which I had become tired, and have since become more tired, notably the pretense of naturalistic illusion.

In *The Long Christmas Dinner* the stage has to have two doors. One symbolizes Birth, an entrance; the other Death, an exit; characters entering the scene are born, they strut their little hours upon the stage and eventually make their exits through a door which, sooner or later, we all have to pass. The stage, then, represents life. Its only furniture is a long table spread for Christmas dinner—the feast of life.

That struck me as a great way to present a play. I bought the printed text, liked it as much as the performance, and bought the author's other dramatic work, a book of short plays called *The Angel That Troubled the Waters*. These seemed to me no less interesting, congenial, and original than *The Long Christmas Dinner*.

Some of them were written to be acted, some of them for what is called the study. Two at least of them still seem to me masterpieces of their kind: *The Happy Journey From Trenton to Camden* and *Pullman Car Hiawatha*. Again they discarded naturalistic illusion in favor of symbolism; but a symbolism which is not at all pompous or pretentious, but is, on the contrary, extremely simple and full of a dry, rather Puritan humor.

Yet none of these works could truthfully be regarded as likely to hit the jackpot of popular favor. In [many] years of effort I have

"The World of Thornton Wilder" by Tyrone Guthrie. From *The New York Times Magazine* (November 27, 1955). © 1955 by The New York Times Company. Reprinted by permission of *The New York Times* and the author.

persuaded people to let me stage two of them. *Pullman Car Hia-watha* we got up in Liverpool as part of a summer course in drama. In a drill hall or badminton court or skating rink relatives of the cast applauded the single and private performance. *Love and How to Cure It* was presented professionally as a curtain raiser to *Candida*. It had a successful tour and London run and was excellently acted. But I think the public only came to see a Mother-Goddess Film Star in the role of Candida.

The next Wilder play I saw was *Our Town*. I had already read and greatly admired the script. Before the commercial production in London it had already been seen in a production by and for GI's which played a limited number of private performances. These I did not see, but they were the object of great local professional respect and admiration. When, however, the play was finally produced in London by a celebrated American director and a good American cast, it was a failure. Critics damned it and the public stayed away in considerable force.

I am convinced that this failure had nothing whatever to do with the quality of the play. Some adverse criticism has been heard of certain aspects of the performance, but my own opinion is that it failed for reasons solely connected with the particular time when it appeared.

It came just after the end of the war. London had had more than five years of danger, hardship, blackout and all-pervading "austerity." What people then craved of the theater was an escape into a world of prettiness and elegance and luxury. This period was the peak of the ballet mania.

The right theatrical recipe was ballerinas in pink floating in three-four time through pleasures and palaces to a predestined ending of elegant bliss in the arms of A Prince in White Tights. What Wilder and his collaborators offered were some serious, homely goings-on in front of black drapes; no glamour, and to add insult to injury the goers-on were prosperous, comfy homebodies, quite untouched by bombing or blackouts or food shortages.

I shall never forget the drop in the spritual temperature, the nipping frost of disapproval, which settled upon a small but earnest audience when one of the actresses in the play bade the milkman to leave three quarts of milk next morning. We had for some time been limited to half a pint per person per day. The jealousy was, of course, unreasonable but understandable. The production, in short, hit London at a bad moment.

Since then I have seen several other *Our Town*'s by British companies, which came at a more appropriate moment and so made up in timeliness for what they lacked in authentic American dialect and atmosphere. The play has now established itself, not merely in the English-speaking theater, but all over the world, as one of the hottest modern candidates for classical status.

In *Our Town,* as in his short plays, Wilder substitutes symbolism for naturalism, ritual for illusion, and discards elaborate scenery for a bare stage. A few chairs and a table or two do duty for everything that is needed in the play. The actors do not even have real "props." They pretend to be grinding coffee, drinking an ice-cream soda or tacking a straggling creeper to the wall of a house, with nothing to aid them but their own skill in mime and the imagination of the audience.

It is an essential part of Wilder's theatrical creed that the theater is a place where actors and audience meet in a game—but a profoundly serious game of make-believe; also that the imagination is best nourished on a simple diet. For an audience to imagine a room it is not necessary to erect walls, doors, windows and show a lot of fancywork in the way of furniture and fittings; to imagine that the actors are out of doors it is not necessary that they should appear in front of a heap of junk representing trees and fields and hills and sky. In some plays it is desirable, but it is not necessary. In Wilder's plays, as in those of Shakespeare, Molière, or nearly any of the great masters, other than those of the nineteenth century, it is not even desirable.

Wilder uses the stage not to imitate nature, but to evoke, with the utmost economy of means, a series of images. He claims that a lot of clutter in the form of scenery and properties and "effects" is a positive hindrance to the process of evocation.

This is not to say that plays produced with this kind of economy of means need necessarily look drab and dull. The stage picture can still be interesting and exciting even if it is very simply achieved.

The failure of *Our Town* in London at that particular moment of history does not invalidate the principle of simplicity. Nor does that particular failure invalidate another basic principle of Wilder's writing: he is essentially an American writer, a New England writer, writing about his own environment. Authenticity to this environment is essential if the best results are to be achieved in production. But at the same time his plays are sufficiently true to universal human experience, sufficiently transcend merely local environment and character, to make them acceptable on a cosmopolitan level.

I believe that such a close attachment to, and interpretation of, a particular part of the earth is an absolute essential to any work of art which can ever be of deep or lasting significance. It is one of the paradoxes of art that a work can only be universal if it is rooted in a part of its creator which is most privately and particularly himself. Such roots must sprout not only from the people but also the places which have meant most to him in his most impressionable years.

In Wilder's case the heredity was New England. His father was a typical New Englander and typical of his time in his insistence on the Puritan virtues, upon low living and high thinking. Temperance and continence were strictly and constantly enjoined; there was, evidently, a formidable insistence upon "Thou shalt not." It is possible that, as so often happens, this insistence upon the negative side of virtue turned a family of high-spirited youngsters into exceptionally positive people.

During Thornton's youth the family moved from place to place in a manner far more customary in America than in Europe. The father was for a time United States Consul in Hong Kong, then ran a newspaper in Madison, Wisconsin, then in California. But always and everywhere the Wilders were consciously and purposefully an American family, upholding what they believed to be good American customs, standards, and beliefs.

Thornton contends that up to the First World War, America was a much more homogeneous society than it is now: still predominantly rural, still governed by predominantly rural and Puritan conventions: far less rich than now and less comfortable, but also less plagued with the complexities and neuroses which accompany wealth and comfort. The problems of a highly industrialized urban society then applied to only a minority in American society and were not a major factor in the formation of American character, thought, speech, and behavior. Consequently, what seems to have been a series of extremely diverse environments and a rather rootless childhood was, he contends, in fact not only typically American but consistent to a single pattern.

It is significant that the father conducted the education of the five remarkable Wilder children according to two dominant principles: they must go, the girls as well as the boys, to schools where they would meet not only children whose economic background was similar to their own, but children from homes both far richer and far poorer than their own. Also, that during the period of their education each of them should spend at least one year abroad.

Thornton's year abroad took him to Rome and Paris. After that he became a school teacher in the Midwest, until in his middle twenties he published *The Bridge of San Luis Rey*. This huge success brought both world-wide acclaim and the financial encouragement to give up teaching and become a writer, to give up a settled life and roam the world.

In the theater, Wilder followed *Our Town* with *The Skin of Our Teeth*. In this play, the technical method is more of a compromise. It relies, more than does *Our Town*, upon spectacular effect. In theme also it is more elaborate. It is an allegory about human tenacity, the capacity of the Human Race to survive by the skin of its teeth the various disasters to which flesh is heir.

I like it less than *Our Town* just because it is less simple. The allegory is presented with extraordinary verve and humor. But, in my opinion, the manner rather overwhelms the matter. One admires the dazzling virtuosity, laughs at the jokes, but the emotional aspects of the theme get jostled out of the picture. One cannot see the wood for the trees. All the same, there are some mighty fine trees just bursting with gaudy flowers and rich fruit—some sweet, some bitter; some smooth and some distinctly prickly.

So far in the theater it has had a more successful career than *Our Town*. This, I guess, is because it offers more spectacular and effective opportunities for the leading players to shine. But so far neither has been what is called A Smash Hit. Professional dramatic critics, being but human, are leery about praising the unorthodox: the public rarely shows enterprise when in search of entertainment. Yet these two plays have quietly earned acceptance the world over among discriminating opinion as works of importance. Where the discriminating lead, the herd invariably follows. These are likely contenders for survival long, long after scores of money-making comedies, which the critics commended and the public adored, have reached utter and deserved oblivion.

With Wilder "so far" is an important qualification. His work is not to be measured in terms of immediate popularity. One of his early plays was *The Merchant of Yonkers*. This was first produced in New York in 1940 under the direction of the great Max Reinhardt. It failed. Fourteen years later the author rewrote it, retitled it *The Matchmaker* and produced it in London. This time it was a success and the same production opened the following year in New York.

In *The Matchmaker,* Wilder is apparently aiming at quite another target than in *Our Town* or *The Skin of Our Teeth. The Matchmaker* makes absolutely no attempt to explore new theatrical territory. On the contrary, it is a farce in the most traditional style, making use of many of the familiar devices which have been employed in farce from Aristophanes to *Three Men on a Horse:* mistaken identity, hiding under tables and in cupboards, men dressed up as women, lost purses.

Although at a first glance the technique may seem entirely different from that of his other plays, there is one point of essential similarity: there is no attempt to make the audience accept illusion. Just as in *Our Town* and *The Skin of Our Teeth,* so the audience at *The Matchmaker* is not asked to believe itself anywhere but at the theater.

The author uses the mechanism of the theater not to create illusion but as a constant reminder that the theater is a symbol of life. The stage is the world. The characters are not merely themselves, but representatives of humanity. The elaborate and preposterous "plot" derives not from life, which it but faintly resembles, it derives from the theater.

The theater which is the background of *Our Town* is the bare stage of a theater during rehearsal, and the action is interpreted to the audience by a commentator who is described as the Stage Manager. In *The Matchmaker* the stage is gaily dressed and lighted up in the style which was familiar to our grandparents; and the comment upon the actors is made by the characters themselves in the form of "Asides" to the audience.

In both plays, and in *The Skin of Our Teeth* as well, there is no attempt to pretend that the goings-on are really taking place, that the audience is anything but a group of people who have assembled, not passively to accept an illusion, but actively to take part in a game of make-believe. This is the assumption behind all Wilder's work in the theater; and this is what I principally like and admire.

Thornton Wilder the man? A compactly built person of nearly 70, he is exceptionally uninterested in his appearance and usually looks as if he had just got off a railway coach in which he has traveled for a week.

Like most human beings he is composed of such contradictory traits as would make a character in a play or a novel seem wildly unconvincing. He is probably the world's foremost authority on Lope De Vega; he knows more of history than most history professors; he can talk philosophy with philosophers, painting with painters, music with musicians. There seems to be no book which he has not only read but remembered in vivid detail.

Yet this is no secluded bookworm; it is a wildly gregarious old gossip who likes nothing so much as rushing from party to party. Colorado to Colombo, Stockholm to Buenos Aires, by plane, by train, by boat; from salon to saloon, from ritzy hotels to dockside pubs, talking, talking, talking, talking.

His talk is a low-pitched, incredibly rapid toccata with a flurried counterpoint of gesture. The bony rather square hands endlessly squirm and twiddle and poke holes in the air; and what a second ago was gossip and nonsense has suddenly turned into an immensely vivacious lecture on Plato, or Italian opera in the eighteenth century, or the influence of Joyce and Gertrude Stein, for both of whom he has an admiration which is at once passionate and rational. He is as idiotically stage-struck as a school-girl who has just come back from her first matinee; and at the same time can view the whole theatrical melee, including his own work, with a judge's impartiality and Olympian calm.

He has known almost every celebrated author, artist, musician, actor or intellectual of the day; and he enjoys to fling their names into the torrent, the maelstrom, of his conversation: "As Freud said to me in Vienna . . . I told the President of Harvard . . . When I was in Chicago with Texas Guinan . . . The Pope whispered in strict confidence . . . Woollcott and I in Venice. . . ."

But this is no snob; and there is a stillness at the center of the maelstrom. At the end of a conversation in which Wilder seems never to have drawn breath, he will have a shrewd and tolerant and comprehensive impression of the interlocutor.

I treasure particularly happy memories of him at Stratford, Ontario, where he has been a sort of Honorary Fellow of the Shakespearean Company, attending rehearsals, buzzing like a bee in the actors' canteen, splashing dye onto costumes for plague-stricken Thebans, sitting up far into the night at parties, cross-legged on the floor among the youngsters of the company listening to them with grave attention, drawing them out and pumping them full of philosophy, psychology, religion, gossip, jokes, and just plain, practical horse-sense.

The Comedy of Thornton Wilder

by Travis Bogard

The theater is the natural home of the cliché. Stereotypes of character, situation, and belief which a novelist would be embarrassed to conceive, much less develop, come to their particular fulfillment in the theater. Only at the theater is one treated so frequently to innocent adulteries and guilt-ridden matrimonial triangles, to psychopathic villains terrorizing the incipiently courageous, to drifters questing for mothers who have betrayed them, to homespun philosophers crackling with rural wisdom, to melodramatized conflicts between dark and light, right and left, vice and virtue. Only at the theater is experience formulated in terms of repetitious stylizations of human behavior and accepted with so little effective question.

At its worst, the theatrical cliché beggars insight, heating the theater with false passion, with concepts empty of thought, and with attitudes that have been assumed for the occasion without reference to morality or to psychology. The bulk of drama, prefabricated from this rotten timber, crumbles, and what survives is so jerry-built, so patched and misshapen that it can command no real respect from those to whom art is more than a plaything. The phenomenon of antidrama, Ionesco's *The Bald Soprano,* for instance, indicates the degree of revulsion and contempt which even dramatists themselves feel for a genre which, in large part, is so essentially mindless.

The drama may indeed be dismissed as the subliterary toy of the director and actor who have power to divert audiences in spite of the cliché-ridden script. Yet even the greatest drama is not proof against the cliché. In many instances, major playwrights appear to

"The Comedy of Thornton Wilder" by Travis Bogard. From *Three Plays by Thornton Wilder,* where it appears as the introduction (New York: Harper and Row, Publishers, Inc., 1962). © 1962 by Travis Bogard. Reprinted by permission of the publisher and the author.

find solid timber in the rubble of stereotypical theatrical patterns. The tedious, routine story of the revenger told repeatedly in the late Elizabethan theater peaked in Shakespeare's treatment to *Hamlet*; the sophisticated and cynical man-of-the-world who unexpectedly falls in love—such staple fare of the comedy of the Restoration —becomes Congreve's Mirabel; the wife's choice of a lover or husband—the dusty furniture of so many plays by Arthur Wing Pinero and Henry Arthur Jones—becomes, when Shaw develops it, *Candida*; and the mother-questing hero—that common coin of the American dramatist—becomes in O'Neill's work Eben Cabot and Edmund Tyrone.

The great dramatist uses, rather than avoids, the cliché, turning it into a source of strength for his purposes. He is not dominantly an innovator in his themes or his methods. His novelties are in his attitudes, as with Shaw, his finesse, as with Congreve, his intensity, as with Shakespeare and O'Neill. In an art form partaking of ritual and ceremony, the chief strength lies not in novelty, but in the symbolic patterns which involve playwright, performers, and audience in a kind of communion. Cliché, carefully developed, can serve as myth serves, to establish a basis of belief.

A dramatist must do more than give new names to old situations. He must not merely accept them, but must search them for their human roots. He must fit them into a larger concept of his action so that they do more than thrill cheaply the emotions of the spectator. The best balance sets character as both individual and symbol, exploring in a given situation the dilemmas of the individual man and the meaning he has in a larger scheme of implication. In establishing both the immediate and the general, the cliché character and situation are often serviceable as connecting points, for they base themselves on possible human actions; at the same time, because they have been used in so many dramas, they suggest an archetypical possibility through which the largest significance of the action may be developed.

Thornton Wilder has been highly praised as an innovator, a man who, along with O'Neill, freed the American theater from its traditional forms through his experiments in *Our Town* and *The Skin of Our Teeth*. Quite properly, he may be placed in parallel with Bertolt Brecht as a dramatist who uses the technique of alienation to develop an anti-illusory, openly theatrical theater. In *The Skin of Our Teeth* and many of the short plays which preceded it, there are anticipations of such a seemingly new theatrical style as that developed by Tennessee Williams in *Camino Real*. At some moments, he seems to be writing anti-drama in a manner anticipatory of Ionesco. Yet, at the center of all his dramatic work—indeed almost as its major structural element—lies the cliché.

Compared with his drama, Wilder's novels seem fresh-minted, new conceptions whose effects are not repeated. In his novel *The Woman of Andros* (1930), he describes the return of a dead hero from the underworld to relive an ordinary day in his fifteenth year. "Suddenly, the hero saw that the living too are dead and that we can only be said to be alive in those moments when our hearts are conscious of our treasures; for our hearts are not strong enough to love every moment. And not an hour had gone by before the hero who was both watching life and living it called on Zeus to release him from so terrible a dream. The gods heard him, but before he left he fell upon the ground and kissed the soil of the world that is too dear to be realized."

Wilder developed the same suggestion for the climactic moment of *Our Town,* but in the play when Emily returns from the dead to relive a day when she was totally happy, there is instantly summoned to mind dozens of sentimental dramatic romances such as *The Return of Peter Grimm, Smiling Through,* and J. M. Barrie's *Mary Rose.* In the drama the quality of the novel's situation is altered. What was new becomes stereotyped; and yet, with a paradox that can only be resolved by a consideration of the difference between novel and drama, it is Emily who is remembered, just as it is through his dramas, rather than his novels, that Wilder's reputation has become international.

Wilder's earliest dramatic work was published in 1928, following the success of his novel, *The Bridge of San Luis Rey.* In a volume entitled *The Angel that Troubled the Waters,* he collected sixteen one-act plays, some so brief as to be scarcely visible. Many are less than scenes of five minutes' duration. Were it not that each centers firmly on a moral conflict, the plays would more properly be called "Imaginary Conversations" than drama. Yet, although brief and experimental, they are not trivial.

The scope of their conception is astonishing. The *dramatis personae* of the volume include Christ, Satan, Judas, and Gabriel; a French dancer and her tubercular husband; Mary, Joseph, and Hepzibah, the talkative donkey bearing the Holy Family into Egypt; St. Francis; a great actress and her lover; a mermaid; Ibsen, Shelley, Mozart, and Childe Roland. Scenically, were a designer to take Wilder's stage directions literally, each play would require a setting of staggering expense: heaven, hell, the bottom of the sea, a pool in an oriental mosque. A five-page play called *And the Sea Shall Give Up Its Dead* opens with this stage direction:

> The clangor of Judgment Day's last trumpet dies away in the remotest pocket of space, and time comes to an end like a frayed ribbon. In the nave of creation the diaphanous amphitheater is already building for the trial of all flesh. Several miles below the surface of the North Atlantic, the spirits of the drowned rise through the water like bubbles in a neglected wine glass.

In no way, except in their essential conflict, are the majority of these plays fit for, or intended for, the theater. They are exercises of unusual kinds, which Wilder, as he makes clear in his preface, constructed for his amusement to satisfy his curiosity in matters of literature and humanity. Yet they are the beginning, and their quality should be marked.

Their elaborate production schemes, so disproportionate to their length, reflect an unconcern for the routine practices and limitations of the realistic theater. Stripped of embellishments they reduce to very simple elements: to the "three boards and a passion" called for as a prime dramatic essential by older dramatists. In essence they are most like the dramas of the cyclical medieval religious dramas, uncomplicated in their psychology, deceptively naïve, and permitting, though not requiring, elaborate production schemes.

They are not especially concerned with characterization as that term, post-Freud, has called for intricate exploration of psychological motivation. They center, instead, on situation and the emotion emerging from the conflict it engenders. The externals of character are sufficiently revealed to provide human habitation for emotion and no more. Man is viewed at a distance, *sub species aeternitatis,* and in this long view much particularizing detail drops from him.

None of these short works is cheap or sentimental. A conversation between Mary, Joseph, and their garrulous, spinsterish donkey is saved from frightful excesses of cuteness and sentimentality by its brevity, by its native wit, and by Wilder's refusal to permit his actors to provide the characters with more reality of emotion than his design calls for.

This play, *The Flight into Egypt,* can be taken as typical of Wilder's work, and as anticipatory of his later, more mature dramaturgy. Mary, riding on the donkey Hepzibah with Joseph at her side, carries the Christ child toward Egypt. The donkey, refusing to hurry even when the clashing armor of Herod's pursuing soldiers sounds from the wings, talks incessantly, of her legs and theology and points of interest on the route. Behind her, the scenery unrolls on a revolving cyclorama, like the vistas in the mechanical wonders of a Dime Museum. The Tigris and Euphrates pass by; then the pyramid and the Sphinx; and it is only when the Donkey realizes that Mary carries the child who was born in the stable where she was formerly tethered that she hurries and completes the journey successfully.

Clearly this is dangerous ground for a dramatist. It is a combination of cliché concepts assembled in a way that to audiences trained in realistic theater might seem novel. Yet the treadmill on which Hepzibah walks and the unrolling scenery were staple commodities of the nineteenth century spectacles, such as *Ben Hur*; the balky donkey is comic strip material even today, and the talkative spinster who becomes capable in a crisis is routine theatrical fare. The application of these elements to Christian story is the only novelty, and this, in view of the play's evidently traditional moral, is unimportant.

The effect of the whole when it is produced is exactly as Wilder's scenic description suggested it should be: a charming mechanical toy, which when wound tightly and the proper springs pressed, endlessly reiterates its story. Character does not obtrude on the sense of the remote and the miniature. The machinery of the setting and the cliché characterizations prohibit any particularization. The Holy Family is separated artfully from reality, held at a distance, turned by Wilder's control of the cliché into myth. Compared with the tedious amateurism of many of the experimental one-act plays of the early twentieth century American theater, *Flight into Egypt*, like its companion plays, reveals a young dramatist with an instinctive mastery of theatrical essentials.

In 1931, six more ambitious one act plays appeared in the volume *The Long Christmas Dinner*. It is an uneven volume. Three of the plays, *Queens of France*; *Love, and How to Cure It*; and *Such Things Only Happen in Books* suggest that Wilder made some effort to come to terms with the theater as he found it and to work with relatively realistic techniques. The results are charming in certain romantic details and amusing in their tricks of plots, but the plays seem slight beside such shorter works as *The Flight into Egypt*.

The remaining half of the volume is of a different order. Taking his direction from the first little plays, Wilder affirmed what was to become his characteristic dramatic manner and found ways to increase the emotional and thematic substance without losing scope or imaginative freedom. The plays in question are the title play, *The Happy Journey to Trenton and Camden,* and *Pullman Car Hiawatha.*

Like *Flight into Egypt,* each of these longer plays is a journey play. *The Long Christmas Dinner* does not move in space, but involves a progress through time, as a family's several generations act their typical stories around a Christmas-dinner table—being born, maturing, and dying at a ninety-year-long ceremonial feast. *The Happy Journey* describes a motor trip from Newark to Camden, New Jersey, and *Pullman Car Hiawatha* encompasses a night's train trip from New York to Chicago.

Flight into Egypt, like its companion plays, required an elaborate production scheme to achieve the distance and the freedom in space and time. For these later plays the requirement remains, but the theatrical means are refined and simplified. The primary restriction on space, time, and distance in drama is setting. If there is furniture, it must be used; if people live in houses, they must relate to its windows and doors; if visual reality is desired in a production, then the characters must also seem real and work as real people do, within the bounds of seemingly real time and place. But if this is not the end, then setting and furniture can be dispensed with, and, with a stroke, the problem is solved.

The Long Christmas Dinner has a purely functional setting: the table and chairs of the dinner itself and two portals, one through which characters enter as they are born, the other the portal to death. Setting is here reduced and turned to symbol with a simple theatrical directness reminiscent of the door to the grave in the medieval morality play, *Everyman.* Undetailed and stark, the setting establishes no limit to the play's sense of the passing of years, and it requires no more than token use by the actors whose common mortality is more vital than their traits of character as individuals.

The settings of *Pullman Car Hiawatha* and *The Happy Journey* are more openly theatrical, less symbolic. In these, the stage is stripped. A platform with lights and chairs, plus a few flats to insist visually that the stage *is* a stage replace the trappings of ordinary theatrical illusions. Here, for the first time in Wilder's work, the Stage Manager is brought before the audience to arrange the furnishings, to describe the effect the setting is supposed to have, and to sustain in his own person the concept of non-illusory drama, which permits the plays to describe their journeys.

What led Wilder to develop these devices is less to the purpose than the consequences of such innovations. A boyhood in the Orient had undoubtedly taught him something of the freedom and scope of the oriental drama, and had perhaps conditioned him to the charming utilitarian values of the formalized acting styles and the ubiquitous, visible-invisible functionaries allied to his Stage Manager. Similarly, his interest in theater would have led him to consider the value of the expressionist experiments of the followers of Strindberg. In the same years as he wrote, the theatrical waters were stirred with experiments similar to his. In Germany, Bertolt Brecht was becoming acquainted with Oriental theater and adapting its methods to his style of Epic Theater. In America, the experiments of O'Neill, John Howard Lawson, and many others had suggested the possibility and the desirability of a break from the realistic unities of Ibsen.

Yet, as his first collection suggested, if Wilder were to write drama at all he would have to move toward a nonrealistic dramatic manner. The development of such enabling techniques were essential so long as he held to his attempt to depict the individual in terms that would call to mind the ultimate destiny of all mankind. And this was his theme. In a sense, perhaps, all of Wilder's plays are about the Day of Judgment, imaging human character as a bubble rising to burst on the surface of eternity. There undoubtedly were influences on his experimental style, but, in the last analysis, Wilder's innovations are important consequences of his point of view and of his way of commenting on experience.

The results of the stylistic developments are important. To take *Pullman Car Hiawatha* as a single example: As the train runs westward through the night, like the mechanical Tigris and Euphrates in *The Flight into Egypt,* fields and towns (including Grover's Corners, Ohio) appear and state their relation to it; trackworkers and others concerned with the train's operation step forward to speak their pieces, like graduates of a School of Elocution, awkwardly stilted in speech, paralyzed with stage-fright; and ultimately, guided by the Stage Manager, the hours of the night and the planets pronounce, through wise saws of the ages, a kind of benediction on the train and on its passengers, who restlessly mutter their night thoughts. The sense is of many voices, half heard at a distance, joining in a chorus somehow relevant to man's destiny, somehow in harmony with the singing planets and with a vast but living immensity. In the end, the train does not click along tracks to a purely local destination. It becomes part of the entire westering turn of the earth, part of the movement of life in space.

The production scheme permits Wilder to hold a view of man

that takes into account individual differences, but in the end reduces them in size. Characters are sufficiently drawn to reveal particular human dilemmas, yet nothing that anyone does is important in its own right. Again, the human characters are cliché figures, but as their individual characteristics slip from them, as their passions are shown to be symptomatic of the kinds of emotions each of these kinds of people would feel, and as individual will remains powerless before final destiny, the cliché figures form into a pattern whose sense is of a typical assortment of men and women, no one worthier of attention than any other. Because they are cliché images of men, they hold an anonymity entirely suitable to Wilder's larger design.

This is not to say that man is unimportant in the total design. If anything, his importance is increased in relation to the wide scheme against which he is projected. Man's will, passion, and suffering, however, are not his most important characteristics. Rather, his importance emerges through his relationship with nature's cyclic movement. He is measured by what he touches, rather than by what he does, and these points of wide-ranging contact are only revealed by maintaining the broadest perspective on his action. Through this perspective, the dramatist found his most characteristic means of expressing his sense of life, and it may have been these means, the theatrical cliché combined with a startlingly simplified stagecraft, that permitted him to become—in his full-length plays—the only important American writer of comedy.

In comedy, when it has not been scraped and sharpened by an informing satiric intelligence, man is shown as the inhabitant of a basically benevolent world. The sense is that he lives within a charmed circle where nothing ultimately painful or evil can happen. The man who slips on the banana peel does not damage his sacroiliac, lovers forced to spend a damp and foggy night on the ground in a wood near Athens do not suffer from over-exposure, heartbreak returns to laughter, and *hubris* leads only to a reasoned acceptance of society's norms. The benevolent limits on action and its consequences affect character, as well. The range of emotion in comedy tends to be smaller. Passionate outbursts with far-reaching consequences, pain, even violent excesses of love are gentled, narrowed, reduced in size and kind and rendered more artificial than real.

In Wilder's first full-length play, *Our Town* (1938) the techniques of the comic artist emerge clearly. The characters are limited, held within the benevolent social framework of a turn-of-the-century small town. Their ambitions are unimportant, their suffering is never great and its consequences are muted. They do not quarrel nor lust. They have no thought for their past or their future. They are bounded by reassuring statistical summaries, by familiar occurrences—the night train, the round of the milkman and the paperboy, the homeward stumbling of the drunken organist—and by familiar places—the kitchen, the soda fountain, the graveyard on the hill.

Significantly, they do not look beyond this bounded township at the nation, the world-at-large, nor at the universal scheme in which they figure. They are not inquirers into destiny, and it is clear that nothing they say or do will ever attempt to alter the nature of things. Instead, they maintain the daily, pious rounds of activity, keeping place within set limits. The result is that they are not called upon to express passion of any violent kind, nor are they permitted to cry out in pain. Wilder removes from his stage even scenes of sickness, although instances are reported in passing. Thus, without important action of will, curiosity, or awareness, Wilder's characters are brought to a condition of emotional gentleness. At its farthest range, their wonder achieves only a childlike awe at the concept expressed in an envelope's address:

> Jane Crofut
> The Crofut Farm
> Grover's Corners
> Sutton County
> New Hampshire
> The United States of America
> Continent of North America
> Western Hemisphere
> The Earth
> The Solar System
> The Mind of God

To Rebecca Gibbs, who tells of the letter, what is most remarkable is that "the postman brought it just the same."

It is odd, perhaps, that these inherently docile creatures, incapable of heroism or villainy, are not to be blamed for refusing to attempt to shape their destinies, but Wilder protected his villagers from a charge of spinelessness partly by admitting no occasion to test them. Later, in *The Skin of Our Teeth*, where every moment is a crisis of huge dimension, Wilder buries the individual response in farcical vaudeville, again relieving the characters from becoming involved as individuals in any moral or spiritual dilemmas. What is left in *Our Town* moves perilously close to the sentimental, and would perhaps commit itself irrevocably to saccharine patriotic images were it not that Wilder measures humanity from a distance.

The essential difference between *Our Town* and the bulk of American folk drama is that Wilder attempts to convince no one of his truth by insisting that what he presents is the reality itself. If his story had been developed realistically, carefully plotted, decorated so as to attempt to convince the audience that it was seeing living human beings, much of its truth would have drained from the play, and all of it would have seemed sentimental and unconvincing. But Wilder, as his earlier plays suggested he might, avoids this and with it much of the fraudulence of American folk drama. He insists that the actors are only pretending to be characters. They are stage-managed; they are in rehearsal, so to speak. Above all, they are not attempting to convince anyone of the reality of their illusionary comings and goings. They are deliberately depicted as theatrical stereotypes.

The result is that Wilder's characters become emblems of reality, not reality itself. They are there to remind audiences of familiar things in whose recognition there is pleasure and security. Like the statistics quoted in the opening sequences of the play, the things the characters do are ways of naming blessings.[1] The characters seem a little like priests, the guardians of a shrine whose rituals they only dimly comprehend. In their appointed rounds, they touch familiar things and receive a kind of blessing from the act. They are secure in eternity, and what they do is a ritual enactment of realities which do not need analysis. And because they are deliberate artifices, they escape the merely sentimental. What they touch has the power of a propitiatory charm, a tribal totem, warding off any invasion of evil or doubt.

The distance provided by the artifice permits the drama to move through broken scenes, fragmentarily tracing the lives of George and Emily and their families and their neighbors. Its primary emotion is the joy of discovery and remembering the discovery of the limited world. Moving backward and forward in time and place, the scenes form, in the end, a whole and describe man's course in

---

[1] Detailed biographical evidence is lacking in substantiation, but his plays suggest that Wilder himself touched reality as firmly and as often as he could. For instance, in *The Happy Journey to Trenton and Camden* he names a high school principal, Mr. Biedenbach, who was in fact the principal of the Berkeley (California) High School which Wilder attended. In the same play, the characters pass and comment on the Lawrenceville Academy where Wilder was teaching as he wrote the play. A sudden blurring of artifice and reality occur, as if the characters were watching Wilder watching them.

the timeless cycle of eternity. Even the moment of greatest agony, when Emily returns to earth and cries out that man is unaware of joy as it passes, diminishes in the free slip of time. Tears drain into the earth and memory lies light as the flesh disappears and as thought releases its hold on dead limbs.

For an audience, this is the value of the play: that it reminds men of the good underlying their hesitation, doubts and agony. It promises no salvation, but, equally, in *Our Town* no one is damned. Wilder does not deny the reality of suffering, the necessity of questing and inquiry, but he sees that all such passion and acts of will shall pass away in the surcease of eternity.

In *Our Town*, the open theatricalism acts to diminish the sentimental cliché latent in the subject matter in much the same way that the convention of the boy actress permitted the artificial and improbable plotting of *As You Like It* to become effective. Character is kept at a distance by the stress on the theatrical means. In *Our Town*, the device obviates the necessity for sustained narrative and, while still permitting character to move and to hold an audience's interest, reduces it to something like norms of the experience Wilder is presenting.

In *The Merchant of Yonkers* (1938), Wilder experimented with another device for attaining the same end. Based on Johann Nestroy's *Einen Jux will es sich Machen*, a German adaptation of a nineteenth century English farce, John Oxenford's *A Day Well Spent*, the play might well be called the Complete Farce, centering on farce's basic concerns, folly, money, and love; developing its story with complex and improbable plotting; filled with "screen scenes" involving sudden discoveries and disguises; and with characters brought on stage for the primary purpose of engineering the story to its close. Even in his use of typical nineteenth century stage costume, Wilder is trying to make his play a reproduction of an older style of dramaturgy. He succeeds so well that the play seems as good as any of its models; unfortunately, it seems no better. Old-style farce permits him to use cliché figures cleverly, and to stress the theatricalism which seem an essential part of his theatrical style. Yet in the empty trivialities of the story, the amorous escapades of the Merchant and his apprentices, Wilder deserts the long view of the human scene which justified the similar effects in *Our Town*. Farce, as farce always does, diminishes humanity, belittles the human scene, and commits itself only to the mechanics of laughter. *The Merchant of Yonkers,* even under the direction of the noted

German producer, Max Reinhardt, failed when it was first produced. Engaging as it was, set against *Our Town* it meant little because its effects were produced for so little purpose.

The farcical theatricalism of *The Merchant of Yonkers* was combined with the more purposive antirealistic techniques in Wilder's next play, *The Skin of Our Teeth* (1942). *Our Town*'s stage manager is banished behind the wings, to be sure, but his anxious voice is heard in moments of production crisis, and his presence is felt everywhere. As in *Our Town*, the audience is continually reminded of itself by intrusive voices from the auditorium, by ushers participating in the destruction of the theater to "save the human race" from the Ice Age, and by the many kinds of free vaudeville which occur in the action. From backstage come dressers and stage hands to duplicate the passing of the planets and the hours, as in *Pullman Car Hiawatha*, and the swaying flimsiness of the scenery continually stresses the essentially illusory nature of the theatrical experience.

Added to this is the element of ancient theatrical farce, notably in Sabina's opening and closing soliloquy, where she is permitted to enact the part of the traditional comic maid delivering the exposition. The effect is to dispel illusion in a burlesque of antiquated stage conventions which emphasizes continually the theater's false face.

As in *Our Town* and, to a lesser extent, *The Merchant of Yonkers*, the devices minimize the particular psychology of the characters, turning them into figures in a charade who perform before a symbolic setting a deliberately unconvincing enactment of man's progress through the ages. Again, the temporal and spatial freedom permitted by the setting enables the action to move in fragmentary symbolic configurations forward and backward in time.

The Antrobus family is several specific families: it is the family unit of the cave-dwellers; it is Adam, Eve, Lilith; it is the family of Noah; it is the family of the average present-day suburban commuter. Its many specific identifications, however, combine to make it the archetype of all families in all times. It becomes "Every Family," the norm of the concept, much as the configurations in *Our Town* become norms. All images are blended in a composition of universal significance.

Thus far, Wilder develops what he has done before, holding his characters at a distance, that they may become symbols. But now, perhaps taking a hint from the stage manager's relations to his actors in *Pullman Car Hiawatha*, he also stresses that his actors are in fact actors, and he does with them what he had not done in *Our Town* or *The Merchant of Yonkers*—he gives them personal stories to enact within the larger frame of the drama.

The effect is a little like the infinity to be found in barbershop mirrors: Lilith, the eternal temptress, is a maid named Sabina, who is played by an actress named Miss Fairweather, who, in turn—once this aperture has been opened—was played by an actress named Tallulah Bankhead. Essentially a comic device, refined and put to more significant service than usual, the technique is similar to that which Shakespeare developed with his original Rosalind: a boy, pretending to be a girl, pretending to be a boy, pretending to be a girl, to the ultimate negation of any reality of character.

In Wilder's play, the device allows him to maintain the sense of comedy even when he portrays situations involving world cataclysm. Yet it is also true that this illumination behind the mask tends at certain points in the action to increase the audience's sense of identification with his characters at the same time that it maintains the long view. At its easiest level, the play has the delights of vaudeville. Thus, when Miss Bankhead read the line, "The Ten Commandments, faugh!" and added in a throaty aside what was evidently a deep personal conviction, "That's the worst line I ever had to say on any stage!" the Bankhead personality broke through layers of Fairweather and Sabina with an effect reminiscent of Hogarth's drawings of false perspective.

Not only serviceable for comic purposes, the device provides Wilder with the empassioned climax of his play. In Act III, when Cain's murderous frenzy becomes the actor's reality, when the artificial enactment of a symbolic gesture becomes the particular actor's truth, illusion and reality merge in a way that neither negates the effect of the passion nor permits the passion to come too close so as to destroy the essential perspective of the play. It is Wilder's particular ability to superimpose artifice on reality in this way, projecting life through his imagery.

In the end what Wilder achieves by his technical experiments with point of view and identification is freedom to depict man moving in great gaps of time, of the limited terrestrial animal who has a dim vision of eternity and, because of it, somehow musters the will to survive.

After *The Skin of Our Teeth*, Wilder turned to matters other than the stage[2] until 1954, when his rewritten version of *The Mer-*

---

[2] Omitted from consideration here are his early play, *The Trumpet Shall Sound* (1927), his translation of Andre Obey's *Lucrèce* which Katherine Cornell played

chant of Yonkers opened under its new title, *The Matchmaker*. As directed by Sir Tyrone Guthrie, the play, no longer overshadowed by the success of *Our Town*, came into its own as an amiable piece of tomfoolery. The revisions are very slight, amounting in effect only to the kind of judicious pruning and tightening which any play may expect to undergo in production. At only one moment does Wilder make a significant alteration. Mrs. Levi's soliloquy at the end of Act IV which begins "Ephraim Levi, I'm going to get married again . . ." contains in its original version a lengthy analysis of the people who refuse to accept the human race:

> You and I have known lots of people who've decided—like Horace Vangelder—not to live among human beings. Yes, they move about among them, they talk to them, they even marry them; but at heart they've decided not to have anything to do with the human race.
> They become secret.
> They ask nothing and they give nothing.
> They've refused the human race and perhaps they're right.
> And the first sign that a person's refused the human race is that he makes plans to improve and restrict the human race according to patterns of his own. It looks like love of the human race, but believe me, it's the refusal of the human race,—those blue-print worlds where everyone is supposed to be happy, and no one's allowed to be free.
> If you accept human beings and are willing to live among them, you acknowledge that every man has a right to his mistakes. . . .

The lines state clearly enough one of Wilder's creeds, and perhaps provide a partial explanation of his insistence that man is better off not knowing the nature of his destiny. Yet they are repetitious and overly explicit, and in their sociological implications a little heavy for the tone of the farce.

In the revision, the lines are altered:

> After my husband's death I retired into myself. Yes, in the evenings, I'd put out the cat, and I'd lock the door, and I'd make myself a little

---

in 1932, and his version of the Alcestis story, variously titled *The Alcestiad, The Drunken Sisters,* and *A Life in the Sun.* The latter was first staged at the Edinburgh Festival in 1955, but was withdrawn from the English stage thereafter. It has been published in German translation. Its first general appearance in English was as the libretto of an opera by Louise Talma. Wilder has been at work for some years on two cycles of one-act plays concerned with the Seven Deadly Sins and the Seven Ages of Man. When completed they are intended to be played in varying combinations over a series of evenings. Three of these plays were staged off-Broadway in 1962.

rum toddy; and before I went to bed I'd say a little prayer, thanking God that I was independent—that no one else's life was mixed up with mine. And when ten o'clock sounded from Trinity Church tower, I fell off to sleep and I was a perfectly contented woman. And one night, after two years of this, an oak leaf fell out of my Bible. I had placed it there on the day my husband asked me to marry him; a perfectly good oak leaf—but without color and without life. And suddenly I realized that for a long time I had not shed one tear; nor had I been filled with the wonderful hope that something or other would turn out well. I saw that I was like that oak leaf, and on that night I decided to rejoin the human race.

The difference is partly in the tone, in the use of the concrete rather than the general, but mostly in the quality of the imagery. In its stress on growth and on the value of life, the imagery of this one speech is almost sufficient in itself to lift the farce from its emptiness, to turn it in the end to comedy.

Comedy should be distinguished from farce in two respects. First, it is not centrally satiric. Comic satire in drama always results in farce. In plays by Aristophanes, Ben Jonson, Molière, and Shaw, the generic form which their satire develops is that funny pattern of humanly improbable action where event is significantly separated from character. The work of Beckett and Ionesco has taught the playgoer once again that farce is capable of serious statement. As all drama can be, farce is a way of looking at life, and at times its particular distortions have no equal for reflecting an inherently distorted world. But farce in the hands of a great playwright is possessed by a demon. It is raised from a sterile existential hell and forced to caper insanely before laughing multitudes. In itself it generates no emotion. An audience for farce is a little like the farce itself—possessed by the attitudes of the playwright. The emotion is applied to the work, not developed within it. An audience is called to share Aristophanes' ribald rage and Molière's scorn but not primarily to understand or sympathize with the characters. What the characters mean is more important than what they do, because their every action only reiterates their hopelessness and their folly. With Ionesco, farce again antiseptically applies a styptic to emotion; with Beckett, although farce is often betrayed by sentimentalism, the end result is more likely to be a sense about Gogo, Didi, and Krapp than a feeling for them.

A second distinction between comedy and its grotesque counterpart follows from the first: that comedy is essentially positive and optimistic, whereas farce is negative in its view of the human condition. Its soulless comedians are generally not permitted any higher good than the merry and notable frauds of Aristophanes' Pisthetairos or Jonson's Volpone. Its world is the artificial construct of the cozener, tales told by a con man to deceive and delight. Whether the cheater be active for love, money, or both, in the end his actions ask no further commitment than that his audience share the dramatist's point of view toward the absurdity he has imaged onstage. The dramatist's truth is local and particular, framed in relationship to temporal criticism and manners, and his characters live, if at all, because folly persists, and in all times cheating is the immediate consequence of folly. Without these particular polarities, so essential in *The Matchmaker,* farce dies and is forgotten despite its wit, its structured cleverness, its frail memorials to the laughter of the dead.

But comedy is a testament to life. Its commitment is to the great regenerative cycle, following man's course from birth through nature to death. By no accident, comedy's main concern is often with love, courtship, and marriage. Comedy's laughter rises from the complications of wooing and of man's stumbling efforts to dominate the life process which grips him. In the great Shakespearean comedy, the laughter arises when the lovers for one reason or another pull away from nature, out of the cyclic process: when the girl destined for love disguises herself as a man, when a woman in obsessive mourning walls herself and her garden away from love. Such spinsters—Olivias, Violas, Rosalinds—and their masculine counterparts, the determined bachelors—the Berownes and Benedicks—as they separate from life, become guilty of folly and move, ironically enough, in the sterile patterns of farce. So Congreve's Mirabel and Millamant, before they "dwindle" into matrimony, move in a maze "like a dog in a dancing school." Yet nature and comedy make short work of the would-be farceurs, overwhelming them in the end and tossing them back to the living source of their blessing, to love, and its vital fulfillment.

It is truistic to acknowledge that in the twentieth century there has been no tragedy to compare with that of the Greek and Renaissance theaters. Often, the most serious criticism of both the contemporary theater and contemporary man is that they are incapable of tragic perception. Yet the point may equally well be made that there is today no comic perception either—a point which may suggest that unalloyed comedy and tragedy are alike in their central point of view and in their final assertion. Although comedy finds its fulfillment in life and tragedy its fulfillment in death, weddings and funerals celebrate the same natural process and both ceremonially testify to the value of the force and of the lives it controls.

For reasons apparent to any watcher of twentieth century skies, such unqualified testimony, such essentially religious testimony as tragedy and comedy have traditionally offered cannot be easily found or readily accepted. The ceremonials which signify joining with or separating from life bring little assurance of sanctity. Men marry and die in haste, and comedy and tragedy have lost their affirmative assurance of life's lasting fulfillments. Both have been hollowed out with farce and sentimentality leaving the form of the thing without its essence, a partial and adulterate perception lacking boldness and wisdom. At the best, a few dramatists have sought after modern equivalents of the tragic and comic values in mixed forms, which by their very impurity testify to the puzzling complexity of an irresolute, modern evaluation of life.

Thus far, in twentieth century American Drama, only two playwrights have proved durable beyond their season. In Eugene O'Neill, there developed a tragedian of stature—awkward, gifted with a giant's strength, sometimes guilty of using it like a giant, yet an artist who saw with the clarity occasionally granted to the pessimist the way man's life can be justified through suffering. At the same time, and conveying something of the same sense of being a little out of the stream of the main direction of American drama as O'Neill's work conveys, Thornton Wilder wrote the three plays which have adhered most closely in this country to the traditional vision and the affirmative concept of great comedy.

In a foreword to *The Angel that Troubled the Waters,* Wilder revealed clearly why this is so. He wrote:

> The art of literature springs from two curiosities, a curiosity about human beings pushed to such an extreme that it resembles love, and a love of a few masterpieces of literature so absorbing that it has all the richest elements of curiosity. I use the word *curiosity* in the French sense of a tireless awareness of things. It is too late to arrest the deterioration of our greatest English words. We live in an age where *pity* and *charity* have taken on the colors of condescensions; where *humility* is foolishness and *curiosity* is interference. Today *hope,* and *faith* itself, implies deliberate self-deception.

Wilder is right, of course. The sympathies which came so readily and strongly to men in the past are now perplexing and adulterate, unable to abide questioning. Eugene O'Neill constructed an entire scheme of tragedy on the hope that implies deliberate self-deception.

Yet Wilder, as his revision of Dolly Levi's soliloquy suggests, is not quite willing to give over the polarities of past assurance: pity, charity, humility, simplicity, hope, faith, and the curiosity that leads to wonder. That he cannot deal with them as they essentially are but must cast them in terms of cliché images from old theatrical modes is a consequence of the human condition, not a necessary element in Wilder's faith. Of his first plays he remarked that they are almost all religious plays, but, he added, "religious in that dilute fashion that is a believer's concession to a contemporary standard of good manners."

The concessions must be made. Perhaps, in dealing with religious themes in theatrical terms they have always to be made. Yet it is evident that the concessions are in the form of technical experimentations, of the way of presenting the themes, rather than in the themes themselves. At the center of his dramas, at least, Wilder makes no concession. That he does not explains much of his present pre-eminence and suggests why his work may survive the more ephemeral drama of his time.

The Men-Taming Women
of William Inge:
The Dark at the Top of the Stairs

by Robert Brustein

The Dark at the Top of the Stairs is William Inge's fourth play to be produced in New York. It is being extravagantly hailed both by critics and the public as another major achievement in the substantial canon of a developing playwright, keeping Inge's star firmly fixed in the small pantheon of Broadway's top dramatists. Unlike the other members of Broadway's triumvirate, Tennessee Williams and Arthur Miller, Inge has never had a critical or box-office failure, and the three movies made from his earlier drama—*Come Back, Little Sheba; Picnic;* and *Bus Stop*—have ranked high among the top grossers of all time. Considering the modesty—one is tempted to say the mediocrity—of his work, it is clear that the excitement over Inge has been inspired by something other than the intrinsic value of his plays.

One explanation may be that Inge is regarded as Broadway's first authentic Midwestern playwright. The theater up till now, treating the Midwest as a large mass of unidentified land west of Sardi's and east of Schwab's drugstore, has been content to celebrate only the wholesomeness of the area, usually in song and dance. New England has denoted incestuous family life and the Puritan conscience; the South, tortured libidos and crumbling institutions; New York City, the glitter of witty high life and the social unrest of idiomatic low life. But the Midwest has always, in its Broadway stylizations, remained free from the complexity and suffering of

"The Men-Taming Women of William Inge: *The Dark at the Top of the Stairs*" by Robert Brustein. From *Seasons of Discontent* (New York: Simon and Schuster, London: Jonathan Cape, Ltd., 1965). Originally published in *Harper's Magazine* (November 1958). © 1958 by Robert Brustein. Reprinted by permission of the publishers and the author.

those areas. Rodgers and Hammerstein exalted it, in *Oklahoma!*, as a joyous zone of calico gowns, scrubbed blue jeans, and homogenized souls, while Meredith Willson recently identified it, in *The Music Man*, with big brass bands, "Ioway stubbornness," and ingratiating con men.

Inge, on the other hand, seems to have restored to Midwesterners their privilege to be as traumatized by life as any other Americans represented on Broadway. His characters, suffering in a purgatory of low-pressured "realism," adamantly refuse to twirl their skirts, burst into song, or ripple with good feeling. A closer look at his work, however, reveals that beneath the naturalistic dirt and cobwebs lies a view of man as blandly nerveless as that held by Rodgers and Hammerstein—and more sinister since it robs the individual of his aspiration, his heroism, and even his manhood.

Wandering aimlessly in a number of directions, *Dark at the Top of the Stairs* chronicles the fortunes of the Floods, a middle-class family living in an Oklahoma boom town in the early twenties. Concerned primarily with the crises of daily life, the play is conscientiously unheroic. The only climax it can boast hinges on an improbable turn of plot, the suicide of a Jewish boy who has been insulted at a country-club dance; the only plot concerns the breakup and reconciliation of the mother and father after a spat over the cost of a dress. There is practically no action; the crucial scenes all occur off stage (Inge uses the Messenger device as extensively as Euripides). The play moves, if at all, by a series of character revelations, and the dialogue, in keeping with the unheroic line of the play, is dry, repetitive, and monotonously folksy.

Over the placid lake of this play, Elia Kazan hurls thunderbolts. His production is in a state of carefully controlled frenzy. Pat Hingle as the father shouts his lines so vigorously that one expects him to be answered from the house across the way; Eileen Heckart, though vastly amusing, is miscast as the aunt and bawls her part in the brash, busy accents of musical comedy; the daughter's flapper friend sibilates her hissing consonants, exposes her bloomers to her date and lifts her leg into her skirt on gag lines as if she were playing the soubrette in *The Boy Friend*. Where Inge indicates a tight bond between mother and son, Kazan slams home all the incestuous implications; where Inge indicates plainness in the daughter, Kazan casts a conventional stage adolescent with the face of Corliss Archer and the look-at-me-I'm-radiant speech of Julie Harris. Inge proposes calm and lassitude, Kazan imposes theatrical high jinks. What with all the nut-cracking, chicken-eating, behind-patting,

jewelry-fingering, shoe-shining, sewing, crying, stuttering and yawn-
ing that goes on, his characters are rarely empty-handed or empty-
mouthed—and in a play almost devoid of climaxes we are served a
climax every five minutes. The period set and the period costumes
seem strangely alien elements amidst these tempestuous goings-on.
Only Teresa Wright as the mother, quiet-voiced, tiredly pretty,
lined with anxiety, seems to belong among the faded daguerreo-
types of this old house.

Kazan's treatment of the play shows his understandable impa-
tience and bafflement with it. *Dark at the Top of the Stairs* drones
on like a Midwestern cricket, making no powerful statement, dis-
playing no moving action, uttering no memorable dialogue. Although Inge had previously gestured toward Kazan's brand of high-
pitched drama, with a naturalistic play about reality and illusion
(*Come Back, Little Sheba*), a satyr play glorifying the phallic male
(*Picnic*), and a vulgar folk vaudeville with night-club acts and dirty
jokes (*Bus Stop*), here he has created a nostalgic tribute to his childhood in that most tenuous of Broadway forms, the mood-memory
play.

The play is dedicated to Tennessee Williams but it is the first
of Inge's works not to be largely dominated by Williams' personality. In fact, *Dark at the Top of the Stairs* yields little personality at
all. Inge is becoming so detached from his works that he does not
even contribute a style to them. Here he carefully distills his facts
and memories until they acquire a vagueness which robs them of
anything personal or immediate except the author's sympathy. The
effect is that of affectionate reminiscence. We are meant to be
shielded from the world's glare, not blinded by it; we are to be
cradled in the bittersweet security of family life. Seen through the
eyes of the ten-year-old protagonist, the world of trouble loses its
threat—the most dire events have a happy resolution and even
our most intense fears (our fear, for example, of darkness near the
door of our room) are dispelled when we can ascend the stairs on
Mama's arm. How could the director of *Death of a Salesman* and
A Streetcar Named Desire, the anatomizer of psychological turbu-
lence, see this work other than as something he must "keep going"
and make recognizable to the audience which views it?

Despite the smoke screen sent up by the production, one can
agree with the critics that this is Inge's best play. He has finally
acknowledged that he is dealing with a quiet family theme (his
genre is domestic romance) and thus can partly dispense with the
souped-up vitalism, the artificial melodramatics, the seedy natural-

ism and the ambiguous symbolism that marred his other more
theatrical work. But if *Dark* is better than his other drama this is
because it is more honest, not more original. The play reinforces
my opinion that Inge is a dramatist of considerable limitations
with a very small gallery of characters, situations, and themes.

Inge follows Williams in writing she-dramas, in giving to women
if not the leading then certainly the pivotal (and most insightfully
created) role in his work. Inge, however, concentrates more on the
pathos of the woman's suffering and, unlike Williams, permits this
suffering to issue in triumph. Although the central conflict is a
struggle between man and woman, the woman's victory does not
necessarily posit the man's defeat. Rather he capitulates, giving
himself up to the woman's power to comfort and provide his life
with affirmative meaning. Thus Inge's plays end—like most romances—in marriage or reconciliation.

Specifically, Inge's basic plot line revolves around a heroine
threatened either with violence or sexual aggression by a rambunctious male. Both terrified and attracted by him, she tries to escape
his influence until she learns that, despite his apparent confidence,
he is riddled with doubts, loneliness, and need. Once he has con-
fessed this, he loses his ogre quality and the woman is able to
domesticate him without difficulty. In *Come Back, Little Sheba,*
the plaintive good-natured frump, Lola, is threatened with a
hatchet by her alcoholic husband. Though she tries to leave, she
is reconciled to him when, returning from the hospital, he indicates his helpless need of her:

> Doc. (*Tears in his eyes, he all but lunges at her, drilling his head into
> her bosom.*) Honey, don't ever leave me. *Please* don't ever leave me.
> . . . Please forgive me. . . . And I'll try to make everything up.
>
> Lola. (*There is surprise on her face and new contentment. She becomes
> almost angelic in demeanor. Tenderly she places a soft hand on his
> head.*) Daddy! Why, of course I'll never leave you. . . .

Picnic, Bus Stop, and *Dark at the Top of the Stairs* present the
situation of the helpless child-man and the comforting mother-
woman in progressively disguised form. In *Dark,* Rubin Flood and
his wife Cora dispute over his reluctance to assume the responsibilities of married life. She accuses him of infidelity, drinking, and
indifference toward the children while he charges her with trying
to inhibit his freedom. After slapping her and leaving the house
in a fury, Rubin later returns to apologize and to confess his fears
of the future. Heartened to learn that a self-possessed man like

Rubin could fear, Cora encourages him to bring his problems to her and the play ends on a note of mutual compromise. The dark which has always enveloped the top of the stairs, a source of fear not only to their little son but a symbol of the family's fears, is dispelled by a shaft of light on the naked feet of Rubin Flood, waiting for his wife to ascend into his arms.

From this it can be seen that Inge's purpose in writing drama is not political, moral, aesthetic, or social, but rather psychological or, more accurately, homiletic. The pervasive surface theme of his work is that people find salvation from fear, need, and insecurity only through the fulfillment of domestic love. For the men, however, this fulfillment is always accompanied by a sacrifice of a very curious order. Some idea both of the men and their sacrifice is suggested by the following anecdote related in *Picnic:* "Last year . . . some of the [women] teachers made such a fuss about a statue in the library. It was a gladiator and all he had on was a shield on his arm. Those teachers kept hollering about that statue, they said it was an insult to them every time they walked into the library. Finally they made the principal—I don't know how to say it, but one of the janitors got busy with a chisel and then they weren't insulted any more." Most of Inge's heroes have the physical and cultural characteristics of this gladiator, and all of them have a hidden fear of sharing, through their contact with women, his emasculation.

Inge's hero, like Williams', after whom he is modeled, is a member of a new theatrical type that Herbert Gold has called the "male impersonator." Dressed in a conventional uniform of blue jeans, cowboy boots and tee-shirt (which the hero invariable has an opportunity to remove), he is equipped with bulging biceps and enormous sexual potency. He proclaims his manhood in much the same way that Jayne Mansfield proclaims her womanhood, not by evidence of maturity, intelligence, or control but by exaggerated physical characteristics.

Inge emphasizes this further by fitting his hero with some special prowess, usually athletic, which might attract from the American mass audience the same kind of admiration that gladiators enjoyed in Roman circuses. Sometimes, as in the case of the "sated Bacchus" Turk in *Come Back, Little Sheba,* the male's athletic gifts and sexual power are combined in the same symbol. Turk is a champion javelin thrower but the javelin is described in unmistakably phallic terms ("It's a big, long lance. You hold it like this, erect—then you let it go and . . . it sticks in the ground, quivering like an arrow"). For the man who stakes all his claims to masculinity on his muscles, castration fears can be, of course, very powerful. The castration motif is underlined when Doc, in Lola's final dream, takes over from Turk and makes the javelin and all it stands for disappear completely from their lives ("You picked the javelin up real careful, like it was awful heavy. But you threw it, Daddy, clear, *clear* up into the sky. And it never came down again"). After this threat has been removed, Lola, who has up till now been letting her husband fix the breakfast, starts about the business of making his eggs. Significantly enough, she reverts to the wifely role, not like Molly Bloom through her husband's assertiveness, but rather through his declaration of dependence on her.

Hal of *Picnic,* Bo Decker of *Bus Stop,* and Rubin Flood of *Dark at the Top of the Stairs* all combine Turk's athletic and erotic prowess with Doc's dependent fate. Hal, a potential All-American back, is described in the familiar imagery of the phallic fraternity as a boy "stud" and "King Kong." Before the heroine can freely give herself to him, he must sacrifice his sexual and muscular bravado and admit he is only a liar and a "bum." This sacrifice is symbolized by the loss of his boots, introduced earlier as a sign of his militant masculinity. Bo Decker, a rodeo champion, after violently trying to abduct Cherie, cries, apologizes before the company, and indicates his tamed domesticity by solicitously putting his leather jacket around her shoulders. An older man than Inge's usual hero, Rubin Flood was in his youth an Oklahoma pioneer who fought Indians and buffalo. First seen by his wife "riding down the street on a shiny black horse like a picture of Sin," he had such appeal that he impregnated her before they were married. Like all of Inge's males, however, his rambunctious masculinity hides a need for solace and comfort. Rubin, however, is less reluctant than the others to admit why he has to suppress this need: "It's hard for a man t'admit his fears, even to hisself. . . . He's always afraid of endin' up like . . . your brother-in-law Morris." With Morris already characterized as a man henpecked by his wife into "wrecked virility," it becomes clear that Rubin is expressing his fears of symbolic castration. That his fears are groundless is indicated by the ending of the play. Rubin has surrendered *his* cowboy boots also (he leaves them outside the door for fear of muddying Cora's carpet) but awaits his wife in bare feet for the sweet fulfillment of conjugal love.

Thus underneath Inge's paean to domestic love lies a psychological sub-statement to the effect that marriage demands, in return

for its emotional consolations, a sacrifice of the hero's image
(which is the American folk image) of maleness. He must give up
his aggressiveness, his promiscuity, his bravado, his contempt for
soft virtues and his narcissistic pride in his body and attainments,
and admit that he is lost in the world and needs help. The woman's
job is to convert these rebels into domestic animals. If this requires
(as it always does in Inge) going to bed with the hero before marriage she will endure it; and although she may accuse her husband
(as do Lola and Cora Flood) of marrying her because she was
pregnant, she nevertheless has managed to establish the hero's
dependence on her and thus insured that he will remain to provide
for the family. The hero has been made to conform, not to his own
image of maleness but to the maternal woman's. Each of Inge's
plays reads a little like *The Taming of the Shrew* in reverse.

Now it would be hard to quarrel with this if it were simply an
objective and categorical description of relations between a certain
kind of people. The man who hides fundamental insecurities behind an exaggerated show of maleness is a familiar figure in American culture (clearly Inge sees Stanley Kowalski with more psychological depth than Williams) and it is very likely that he will end
up in a filial, dependent relationship with his wife. What is suspect
is the persistence with which Inge presents the same situation. De-
picting this limited brand of healthiness as fanatically as Williams
depicts his limited brand of sickness, Inge seems to ignore all other
possibilities for happy family life. A quick glance at his minor
characters will show that almost everyone in his plays is characterized by their willingness or unwillingness to sacrifice their individual selves to love. The plain self-pitying daughter in *Dark*
astonishingly turns out to be the indirect cause of the Jewish cadet's
suicide because, feeling sorry for herself, she wasn't around to help
him when he needed comfort ("The only time anyone *wanted* me,
or *needed* me in my entire life. And I wasn't there"), while the
poetry-spouting professor in *Bus Stop* owes his unhappiness and his
perversity (he molests young girls) to his inability to subordinate
himself to love ("I never had the generosity to love, to give my own
private self to another, for I was *weak*. I thought the gift would
somehow lessen *me*"). Inge has been accused of giving a sexual
construction to every action, but although he will exploit sex (and
circuses) for theatrical effect he is certainly more interested in the
redemptive power of conjugal or romantic love. Inge visualizes the
world as a mass of outstretched arms, blindly groping for each
other, with every problem resolved in the marriage bed.

Compare Inge's with even the most outlandish enactment of sexual relations (such as Shaw's: "I love you. The Life Force enchants me; I have the whole world in my arms when I clasp you. But I am fighting for my freedom, for my honor, for my self, one and indivisible") and you will see where his most serious limitations lie. John Tanner of *Man and Superman* fights to keep inviolable a self which Shaw has shown us in action, writing pamphlets, arguing socialism, speaking wittily and incisively about the lifeless conventionality of his time; the Inge hero, if he struggles at all, fights to maintain an *idea* of self which is wrong from the start. In marrying, Tanner gives up his individual freedom, not his genius; Inge's hero gives up his one distinguishing characteristic, phony though it may be, the sexual dynamism with which he has caught the attention of the spectator. Thus Shaw's vision opens out onto political and moral horizons; Inge's vision closes in on the family and holds us trapped there within the four walls of the home.

The limited boundaries of Inge's moral and social perspectives are dictated both by his subject matter and his characters. With evil equated with lovelessness, evil by some strange process disappears as soon as its character is explained. Inge needs villains but they never appear on his stage (the anti-Semitic woman of *Dark* is merely spoken about) while whoever on stage has the capacity to cause serious trouble grows harmless as soon as we learn that they too are sad, lonely, and frustrated. Concentrating on motives and causes rather than actions and results, Inge avoids confronting any serious moral issues. Although Inge, by his use of the indirect method in *Dark*, tries to make us think of Chekhov, the differences between the two dramatists are vast. Chekhov always emphasized that sympathetic people can cause evil too, that the harm they do is not palliated but rather all the more terrible for understanding it. Inge's characters labor to become as "well-adjusted" as the audience; Chekhov's characters *are* the audience and reflect its sins and faults ("Have a look at yourselves and see how bad and dreary your lives are"). Thus while Chekhov's impersonality reveals his moral passion, Inge's conceals his secret flattery of the spectator.

Inge lacks Chekhov's social passion as well. The social world for Inge is merely a dim image of outside practically invisible to the family eye. *Dark at the Top of the Stairs* purports to say something about the Midwest's transition from a frontier to a money culture but all it really says is that some people (never shown) got bigoted (they weren't before?) and rode around ostentatiously in expensive cars. Inge eventually escapes the entire issue in the helpless incomprehension of Rubin Flood ("I dunno what to think of things now, Cora. I'm a stranger in the very land I was born in").[1]

This is life without heroism, wit, intelligence, or even true energy, akin in its lack of hard virtues to life as desparingly visualized by Beckett and Ionesco. Inge's mood, however, remains steadfastly optimistic, for with serious problems, other than finding a proper adjustment to love, never threatening, optimism comes easy. It would be unfair to compare this world with the heroic universe of Shakespeare (can you imagine Hamlet, Lear, or Macbeth each solving his dilemma by laying his head on a woman's breast?)—simply try to apply Inge's panacea to the domestic difficulties of Ibsen's Nora, O'Neill's Hickey, or even Miller's Willy Loman. No, Inge can maintain his affirmations only by a simplistic view of life and a careful selection of characters. *Dark at the Top of the Stairs* is Inge's most acceptable play because, seen frankly through the eyes of a child, it makes less pretense at being adult; it is, after all, a child's world where social and moral issues assume no importance and where whatever is dark and evil can be expunged by the comfort of a woman. Although the play has depth, however, it has no width. By Inge's own choice, it wallows in commonplaces. Its most significant statements are like a series of homilies out of the *Farmers' Almanac:* "The people we love aren't perfect. . . . But if we love them, we have to take them as they are"; "Bad people you don't hate. You're only sorry they have to be."

Thus Inge's Midwest, despite its occasional psychological intensity, is not really different from the Midwest of Rodgers and Hammerstein, a land where the gift of milky happiness is obtained when some obstacle ("pore Jud" or resistance to love) is removed. Despite its flirtation with the "dangerous" subjects of modern American drama (sex and violence), Inge's drama is in the end ameliorative, and this fact accounts for his present-day popularity. Inge can hardly be called a "developing playwright" because he merely

[1] Inge's handling of the Jewish cadet also reveals his tendency to evade social issues. Sammy Goldenbaum is too pathetically sweet to be believed. His impeccable manners, his great concern for people's feelings, and his soft stammering speech make everyone else in the play look boorish and, although he is unwanted by his mother (a Gentile movie star—obviously Jews are incapable of behaving badly), he thinks of her with great love and generosity. Inge describes him in exotic terms as a "darkly beautiful man of seventeen" with "something a little foreign about him. . . . He could be a Persian prince strayed from his native kingdom"—Sammy is certainly more Persian prince than Jew. Inge's treatment of anti-Semitism seems very unreal when his subject is neither human nor Jewish.

changes his forms rather than his content. But he does represent a new phenomenon on our stage—he is the first spokesman for a matriarchal America. Inge's family plays constitute a kind of aesthetic isolationism upon which the world of outside—the world of moral choice, decision, and social pressure—never impinges. Although he has endowed the commonplace with some depth, it is not enough to engage serious attention. William Inge is yet another example of Broadway's reluctance or inability to deal intelligently with the American world at large.

The Theater of Edward Albee

by Lee Baxandall

Edward Albee's theater continues to be controversial. The discussion centers around two questions: one has to do with truth, and the other with dramatic structure. The first runs as follows: is the image of human relations in America which Albee presents justifiable because it is in some sense realistic, or is his an essentially flawed and perverted point of view? The second is: are there valid grounds for the invented child in *Who's Afraid of Virginia Woolf* and the confused events which lead to Julian's death in *Tiny Alice,* or is Albee artistically callow and unable to structure a play properly?

The Albee Family America

Affluence is estranging America from her own ideals.
. . . It is pushing her into becoming the policeman standing guard over vested interests.

> Arnold J. Toynbee, *America and the World Revolution*

The play is an examination of the American Scene, an attack on the substitution of artificial for real values in our society, a condemnation of complacency, cruelty, emasculation and vacuity; it is a stand against the fiction that everything in this slipping land of ours is peachy-keen.

> Edward Albee, Preface to *The American dream*

What is the structure of Albee's theater? His characters are definitely interrelated and cohesive from play to play; the heart of

"The Theater of Edward Albee" by Lee Baxandall. From *Tulane Drama Review,* Vol. 9, No. 4 (T28, Summer 1965), 19-40. © 1965 by *Tulane Drama Review,* and reprinted with their permission and the author's.

his technique is an archetypal family unit, in which the defeats, hopes, dilemmas, and values of our society (as Albee sees it) are tangibly compressed. The device of course is as old as Greek tragedy; only the particularity of *this* family is new. The economy of setting forth a concrete conflict to represent more abstract and even essentially undramatizable situations has always attracted dramatists. (Thus, with a sociologist's insight, C. Wright Mills stressed that public issues erupt as private troubles.) In the family, then, a dramatist can still find the conjuncture of biography and history.

Three generations comprise Albee's archetypal family: *Then*, the epoch of a still-dynamic national ethic and vision; *Now*, a phase which breaks down into several tangents of decay; and *Nowhere*, a darkly prophesied future generation. Only two characters are left over from *Then*: Grandma [in *The Sandbox*] and a *paterfamilias* or patriarch who is occasionally mentioned but never appears. These establish a polarity based upon the axis of female and male principles. It has been often remarked that Grandma is the sole humane, generous creature in the Albee ménage. She tries to relate to others in a forthright and meaningful fashion, but at her age she no longer commands the requisite social weight. The others, her offspring, do not want Grandma involved in their dubious lives. They ask her to stifle her "pioneer stock" values. Her pleas that she be put to use—"Beg me, or ask me, or entreat me . . . just anything like that"—are not heeded, because she is of a different epoch. She sums up the inheriting generation: "We live in an age of deformity. It's every man for himself around this place."

The *paterfamilias* represents the dynamic principle of the vanishing generation. In *The Death of Bessie Smith, Who's Afraid of Virginia Woolf?*, and *Tiny Alice*, his function as entrepreneur and primitive accumulator of wealth is described with awe, but he is never seen. [In *Bessie Smith*] he is the Mayor, the capricious tyrant of Memphis, in his time a capable and dynamic figure—"for the Mayor built this hospital"—but incompetent in his senility—"The Mayor is here with his ass in a sling, and the seat of government is now in Room 206." He remains the Mayor from his sick-bed; he continues to wield power, because for his generation to do so is instinctual. Nor do younger persons offer a challenge. The upcoming generation desires nothing better than to serve the Mayor's political machine or to creep to his bedside for small favors. His counterpart in *Who's Afraid of Virginia Woolf?* is Martha's father, the College President. George speaks of him (ironically) as "a God, we all know that"; his mansion is nicknamed Parnassus and the whole faculty does obeisance to an infinitely remote and super-powered figure with a "great shock of white hair, and those little beady eyes" like a mouse's—a man who "*is* the college" and "is not going to die." Miss Alice's fortune was accumulated by a departed father. Time and again, it is the Robber Barons vs. the new Organization Men. The elder generation's male was an energetic asocial titan. As reflected in the *paterfamilias* and Grandma, an American ethos is vanishing, an ethos that was purposive and energetic, regardless of whether its humane or ruthless aspects came momentarily to the fore. And whatever else they were, the announced values were real.

The *Now* generation is also dominated by male and female archetypes. Mommy and Daddy of *The American Dream* are the most clear-cut representatives of this generation. Looking at them from the standpoint of their elders' values, it is apparent that Mommy provides the transitional figure. She, and not Daddy, takes an interest in practical enterprise; she inherits the male aggressiveness. But although she delights in power, she is glaringly incompetent as the moral steward of her generation. Mean-spirited, immoderate, insincere, and inclined to hysteria, Mommy makes up with wildness what she lacks in confidence. Long relegated to a subordinate family function, Mommy cannot instantly acquire leadership qualities. Yet Daddy has abdicated, for some reason not apparent to her, and someone must govern.

Mommy has several variants, emphasizing one or another aspect of her. Thus the Professional Woman of *The American Dream*, Mrs. Barker, provides the grotesque caricature in the Mommy gallery. She makes her way into areas once reserved for men, diminishing as a human being with each triumph. Martha, in *Who's Afraid of Virginia Woolf?*, has the essential Mommy traits but her character is more complex; she understands her errant behavior even as she compulsively continues it. Miss Alice, the capricious possessor of great wealth, is a Mommy too, and although she has an ineffectual impulse to "care" about people, she—like the Lawyer, who counsels her in practical affairs—is "saved by dedication" to the cruel values of her culture and can grow "hard and cold" when Julian's life is at stake.

What this "dedication" can imply, taken to an extreme, is shown by the Nurse in *The Death of Bessie Smith*. Nurse, though not yet married, is the meanest of the Mommies. Her neurotic and anti-intellectual political attitudes add a sinister dimension to the composite Mommy portrait. Nurse admires Franco, whose opinion, like her father's, "counts for something special." And she is sadistic. Having vehemently refused to put her life on a rational basis, Nurse is prone to hysterical outlets. She could tear the tissue of civilization:

> I am sick of everything in this stupid, fly-ridden *world*. I am sick of the disparity between things as they are, and as they should be! . . . I am sick of talking to people on the phone in this damn stupid hospital. . . . I am sick of the smell of Lysol. . . . I am sick of going to bed and I am sick of waking up. . . . I am tired of the truth . . . I am tired of my skin. . . . I WANT OUT!

This is irrational apocalyptic politics: the voice of the bigot and potential fascist. Why does Albee attribute these tendencies to Mommy, who for him symbolizes contemporary power in America? The first dispute over Albee comes to a head here. Does his representation of Mommy really suggest some important truth? Or is it the distorted revenge of an injured man?

In the first place, Mommy as a political symbol is ambiguous. She represents an emergent force in society, and does anyone doubt that women have strikingly improved their social and economic lot in recent years, that they have gained more professional and managerial positions, hold more property, exercise more real control in the home and community? Is it then surprising that a socially advancing group fails to distinguish itself by urbane reasonableness? In every revolution power has been accrued first and its judicious use learned later. On the other hand, is it not likely that Albee wishes Mommy to represent the political tendency of the nation rather than of simply one sex? We are left uncertain, for, because of his reliance on a family myth and the construction he places on woman's role, Albee's political meaning remains somewhat blurred. Mommy may offer a comment upon power in America. Don't we find in American foreign policy some of the traits attributed to Mommy? Didn't America suddenly rise to world power and responsibility during World War II? Didn't it have to adapt suddenly from an isolationist past? And hasn't there been much comment on the transformation from an "inner-directed" to an "other-directed" personality type in America? If this interpretation is substantially correct, judgments made on Albee's lack of objectivity about *women* need qualification, at the least.

Mommy has taken over the male prerogatives; what is left to Daddy? He has none of his predecessors' traits and the variants of his type are defined by whether they oppose the present passively or with active negation; they have no hope for the future. Daddy trails off toward the *Nowhere* generation; it is often unclear whether he is Mommy's husband or son. Indeed he is best discussed in connection with the *Nowhere* generation, since he and they both behave infantilely. The most passive of the Daddies is in *The Sandbox* and *The American Dream;* he no longer "bumps his uglies" on Mommy or disputes her power, except in quibbles which she enjoys. Whether this Daddy is even employed is uncertain. Surely he is not imaginative. His dreams of becoming a senator, winning a Fulbright scholarship, or leaving Mommy's apartment are ludicrous. George, the history professor in *Who's Afraid of Virginia Woolf?*, represents the opposite pole. No less futile practically, he strenuously produces jokes, situations, and other "fun and games" —imaginative avenues away from despair.

Among the younger males the two in *The American Dream* show once again, very clearly, the weight Albee gives to this passive-active axis. Only one of the youths actually appears. The other, we learn, was the identical twin of this "American Dream" and died while an infant, just months after Mommy and Daddy adopted him. Both twins are homosexually oriented, making symbolic comment upon an emasculated and narcissistic national vision. Grandma says that the dead twin had been sensitive, resentful, and indomitable, with a wildness which made him unbearable to Mommy— who at last mutilated the boy's genitals. She would have murdered him, had he not cheated her by dying first. The passive twin is, by contrast, welcome in Mommy's home and, it seems, in her bed.

The other Albee males can be located in relation to these poles. In *The Zoo Story,* Jerry, with a sensibility so unbridled that he eventually destroys himself, is a counterpart of the twin who died, just as the docile conformist Peter is kin to the "American Dream," the twin who lived. The polarization in *The Death of Bessie Smith,* though less focussed, appears in the contrast between an erotically obsessed Intern and an obsequious orderly. In *Who's Afraid of Virginia Woolf?* the conformist Nick is a forecast of triumph for the IBM male. In *Tiny Alice,* Julian is an imaginative saint with a mission, while the other men passively dissolve into their social roles. This is not so terrible for the butler, whose name, after all, is Butler; Albee suggests that the man's genuine capacities (as society has developed them) do not stand in contradiction to the serving role he plays. The situation of the Cardinal and Lawyer is otherwise. Though they are well educated, their personalities are determined by their social roles and they have no names but their functions. These men have in a sense *chosen* to be types rather than individuals; yet the Cardinal is also provided with a biography which might stand as the classic explanation of why Albee's passive males are that way: his father was a "profiteer," his mother irresponsibly whored around rather than instill him with life values. Even his paternity is in doubt. Thus, lacking tangible origins or values, the Cardinal in craven bafflement "worships the symbol not the substance" and takes the Father proposed by the Church. He will in turn perpetuate symbols over substance. There will, of course, be no offspring.

In [*Virginia Woolf* and *Tiny Alice*], a female of the third generation also appears. One is Honey, Nick's wife, who has numerous naïve dodges aimed at getting free of responsibility; no child-bearing or growing up for her! She abdicates, as have the more sensitive Albee males. Albee does not say why Honey follows the road of inner emigration, but one may guess that she is appalled by what maturity would require her to be and do. With the example of Mommy before her, she defends her child-like looks and innocence through doses of unwitting hysteria and knowledgeable abortion: *she* will not further this vector of history! Honey's counterpart in *Tiny Alice* does not appear, but we hear about her from Julian, who was fascinated by her during his years in the asylum. This woman, like Honey, is infertile and at the same time hysterically focussed on pregnancy. ("A woman who, on very infrequent occasions, believed that she was the Virgin Mary.") She calls upon God in erotic cadences, goes into false pregnancy with the belief that she will deliver the Son of God—and dies from cancer of the womb. Symbolically, this is the fate of all who do not choose, as Julian does, active martyrdom—who instead stay with "the same uproar, the evasions" of sterility.

Thus it ends. Albee's American family undergoes anxiety and terrible barrenness as it staggers into decay. A few fugitives detach themselves and seek solutions in aesthetics. They watch a historical dream wither. What is the core of Albee's viewpoint? The generations move away from practicality toward emasculation; away from the energetic but amoral use of power toward an amoral but inoperative use of power. A frightened populace creating illusory values; a country afraid to articulate its genuine but shoddy rules of conduct; and a handful of males stimulated to imaginative activity of a high order. George's mental purview has little in common with Daddy's sigh, "I just want to get everything over with," and the Intern's lewd unrealized fantasies are nearly as alien to him. George's escape into imagination is the sole solution Albee propounds to the national condition.

Out of the Family into Symbolic Transcendence

> I, thus neglecting worldly sins, all dedicated
> To closeness and the bettering of my mind
> With that which, but by being so retired,
> O'er-prized all popular rate, in my false brother
> Awaked an evil nature; . . .
>
> Prospero in *The Tempest*

The form of an Albee play derives from some characters' imaginative power to force events, not toward historically viable solutions, but at least into channels which are telling and satisfying symbolically.

The Zoo Story, Albee's first play, uses this artistic strategy in showing the struggle by Jerry—who has cultivated his sensibility and integrity but has paid for it with social failure—to make significant contact with a man called Peter, who is a success and a conformist. Other forms of contact proving impossible, Jerry at last provokes Peter into causing his death by stabbing. This might be nothing but a brute, desperate act, yet it becomes much more because it is instilled with rich overtones of the circumstances which made Jerry abstain from the social order. He has gone out of the family, and he symbolically transcends it by showing Peter why, through the particulars of his death.

Albee's formal cunning can be seen, beneath the colloquial language and precise detail, in his bold and intricate sense of organization. "Plays are constructed rather the way music is," he has said, and a lifetime love of music and friendship with composers has prepared him for building a strong skeleton under the alluring flesh. For example, the associations evoked by the characters' names in *The Zoo Story* bring out the polarity of these third-generation males. Peter of course is Greek for rock; he is, as Christ bid, the rock on which the institutions stand. (The existentialists depict persons who live inauthentic existences as being the equivalent of stones, rocks, and trees.) Jerry, like Jeremiah, denounces the false gods of his day. Thus we are prepared, by the names alone, for Jerry's dying whisper to the apostle of conformity, "I came unto you . . . and you have comforted me . . . Dear Peter."

Beyond the force of names is the sheer suggestiveness of sounds. Take the handling of the vocal "O." It becomes, by the play's conclusion, an architectonic element. Early, there is Peter's polite and disinterested "Oh?" as he unresponsively answers the importunate Jerry. It is often used, and is a token of his studied indifference to lives presented to him outside routine channels. Half-way through the play, however, Peter in distress switches to "Oh my; oh my." Jerry tosses back, "Oh your what?" and keeps talking—the "Oh" rises more urgently to Peter's lips. Jerry is stabbed, and Peter howls, "many times, very rapidly," "Oh my God, oh my God, oh my God — . . ." in total incomprehension, to which Jerry replies with "a combination of scornful mimicry and supplication," "Oh . . . my . . . God," and dies. A sound has been imbued with the anguish of the conforming man under stress.

Among the medium-sized units in this play, the fable about the landlady and the obscene dog, for example, is built along the lines of a music-hall sketch. Elsewhere in the Albee plays one can discern arias, duets, and fugues. So much is fairly obvious. The *over-all* symbolic construction of the plays is more complex and deserves close attention, still using *The Zoo Story* as our model.

At the start of this section, I quoted Prospero's explanation of how he studied those esoteric subjects for which the world condemned him. The black arts enabled him, in an isolated place away from vested society, to control all events to his hermitic satisfaction. For those Albee characters with extraordinary imaginative powers, matters are similar: in large part they determine the course and outcome of the symbolic actions in which they are willing to participate. Of course, the differences from *The Tempest* are important. The powers granted Albee's figures can be called magical only as a metaphor of efficacy; at the same time, the physical and social sciences have steam-rollered personality so that there seems little left to man's initiative which does not play into the game of those forces that crush integrity and sensibility.

It is in this perspective that Albee chooses heroes who use essentially aesthetic means to improve the quality of their lives. Bessie Smith is a working artist; Julian, Jerry, and George build imaginative worlds which provide meaning. Two other characters, Grandma at the conclusion of *The American Dream* and Jack, who brings Bessie Smith's corpse into a white hospital though he knows she is already dead, are rather ordinary persons who transcend themselves in situations of extreme indignity. Albee opposes these figures to the world of effete conformity—a world, incidentally, much changed from Shakespeare's, which beckoned to nearly every man with seemingly endless possibilities. An era which produced as heroes Tamburlaine, Faustus, Richard III, Macbeth, Julius Caesar, and Coriolanus hardly could bring forth from its greatest dramatist a hero who preferred surrogate to practical triumphs; at least not until the end of his career darkened Shakespeare's view. The notable thing about Albee is that, writing late in the epoch which Shakespeare heralded, from the "island" which some think was the model for that in *The Tempest,* he sets out with the premises on which Shakespeare ended, as though there were no others. The resort to fantasy has become *a priori* to practical living. Man is from birth on that deserted isle— with Caliban.

Jerry, George, and Julian are foremost in having exceptional powers of symbolic transcendence. These powers are in life used at various levels of awareness and skill by many persons, even seeming conformists. Passive noncompliance with certain social norms may, when sustained, amount to symbolic negation. More advanced forms are seen in acts of sabotage: pranks, vandalism, riots, the remains of lunches that Detroit auto workers sometimes deposit in a difficult corner of the cars they make. Works of art may provide a lucid, transformed expression of the impulse. Its point is always not only to relieve frustration but also to mock or make manifest some absurdity or indignity inherent in the situation.

Thus Jerry by his death incriminates the good citizen Peter; Jerry has plotted the entire devious development of the action. Probably he had sought and failed to become a writer. In this instance his talents are cunning: "sometimes a person has to go a very long distance out of his way to come back a short distance correctly," and relentless: "don't react, Peter, just listen." He flaunts his superiority over a man whom society has awarded the merit badges; he hopes also, and quite desperately, to find some understanding from him. Should Peter respond, the bitter conclusions drawn in isolation will be disproved and the rebel can live. Yet Jerry has from the start little hope, and Peter does not admit awareness even when faced with Jerry's major effort, the parable of the dog, which brings forth only an indignant "I don't understand!" To admit awareness would force Peter to change values and reject the status he has dearly bought. He lies. And Jerry, weary of the indecisive encounters with the Peters, decides for once upon an indelible communication. "You fight, you miserable bastard," he cries, "fight for that bench; fight for your parakeets; fight for your cats; fight for your two daughters; fight for your wife;

fight for your manhood, you pathetic little vegetable (*spits in Peter's face*), You couldn't even get your wife with a male child." Each move is calculated. Jerry knows how to dissolve the aplomb of this antagonist, and it is no difficult matter to induce Peter to seize the knife and hold it thrust out while Jerry, running upon it, dies.

There is symbolic richness in this tableau of death. On the face of it, Jerry is relieved of his unremitting conflict with the Peters. The social process of life-destroying forces in stealthy conquest of life-enhancing forces becomes public and accountable; Peter can no longer deny complicity. "You won't be coming back any more, Peter; you've been dispossessed"—robbed of certitude about his way of life. An audience, should it include Peters, vicariously might be as shaken, as dispossessed. This retribution alone can gratify Jerry. He is so set on broadening Peter's awareness that he urges him to gather his wits and flee before a policeman can come, for it would be futile for the Peters of society to punish Peter; his imagination must do the work. Then Peter may no longer be Peter. This is the primary import of the death.

Jerry's violence and his strategy are like those of American urban juvenile gangs. The gang members feel themselves outcasts; with no other outlets, they turn to destructive but significant acts. Two gangs battling for a turf are struggling for something that, like the park bench, in reality can "belong" to neither. And while they, like Jerry, may dislodge Peter with their knives, the victory is Pyrrhic—that is, symbolic.

From another perspective, Jerry's death is erotic. Jerry withdrew from "normal" sex when he rejected conformist social goals, and it seems mixed up in his mind with the other "normal" activities he despises. Occasional sordid contacts with women and daily encounters with his obscene landlady (another Mommy) reinforce his queasiness. Peter's domesticated heterosexuality is part of what affronts Jerry, and as he throws himself onto the blade in Peter's hand he spears himself on erect sex, terrifying and fascinating because institutional. The irony is that Peter's way of life scarcely has prepared him to perform this duty, and he would not have held the blade out if Jerry had not assaulted the root of his honor: property rights. Jerry is the more capable male; in the real encounter he plays the active partner.

The pattern is of deliberate symbolic adventures which unveil repugnant aspects of society and are symbolically satisfying to the doer. Albee develops this pattern in two ways. The less effective is found in *The American Dream* and *The Death of Bessie Smith*. In these plays a situation is slowly built up like a mosaic, and the transcendence is sprung suddenly, at the end. Grandma and Jack provide brilliant curtain effects, but this strategy has a bad effect on the total structure. We do not see the characters develop or change (except for the frantic revelations provided by the arrival of Bessie Smith's corpse) and the nature of the final transcendence is obscure.

Who's Afraid of Virginia Woolf? . . .

The scene is a small New England academic community. Martha is the daughter of the college president and her husband, George, is a history professor. One night they return late from a faculty party and begin an orgy of verbal sado-masochism. After tearing at each other's dignity and illusions, they turn on a new faculty couple, Nick and Honey, whom Martha has invited for a nightcap. Martha takes Nick to bed, but he is impotent; meanwhile George has retreated to the disinvolved recesses of his imagination, from which he is able to kill his and Martha's most precious shared illusion, the myth supposed to provide a measure of symbolic transcendence: that they have a son. In this mayhem, George is the catalyst, determining the nature and scope of their "fun and games" and guiding the pivotal story about the child.

What is the context of George's actions? Is it merely a quaint college town? The stage setting of the New York production implicated the entire American educated community. It showed a tasteful home, with fitted, recessed bookshelves, hi-fi, curtains, fireplace, early American period furniture, oak beams, a wrought-iron colonial eagle, an American flag queerly reversed, an impressionist painting over the mantel—the comforts of modern living side by side with rough-hewn tokens of the revolutionary past, but dominating them: an American House of Intellect. George and Martha are what has become of the Washingtons; they quip that they have lived "over the past couple of centuries" in this place. George is a symptomatic American intellectual, the most lucid of all Albee's heroes and the best adjusted to his predicament. He and Julian are the only Albee heroes employed by an institution of society. As a history professor, he has a wider perspective than the average man. He is an insider as well as an outsider, and his situation permits him—far more than Jack, Jerry, the "American Dream," or

Grandma—to bare the problems of conformists and malcontents equally.

George's practical failures are his own choice. He was not born incompetent. Martha tells an anecdote about George's refusal to join a sparring match with her father, the college president, during the wartime fitness-program days; Martha took a playful poke at George then, and he went down. He has refused to assume the organization-man etiquette that would qualify him as her father's heir-apparent. "He'd be no good at trustee's dinners, fundraising," Martha notes accurately. "He didn't have any personality, you know what I mean?" What really was objectionable was George's insistence on his right to individuality; given the situation, he had little choice but freely to choose futility.

Like the other Mommies, Martha is an apotheosis of consumerism. With her teeth "like a cocker spaniel," she chews up ice cubes, drinks, George, the young men of the faculty. She describes her dilemma with images from the movies:

> Bette Davis comes home from a hard day at the grocery store . . . she's a housewife; she buys things . . . and she comes home with the groceries . . . and she puts the groceries down, and she says, "What a dump!" . . . she's discontent.

Martha isn't stupid. She is capable of criticizing her own actions, and she can be very affectionate. But she can have no realistic hope of becoming more than a Discontent Housewife while her imagination remains derivative. For although the general situation of "liberated" American women depends on no one woman, it is only through concrete analysis of her own life that any one woman can escape Martha's indefinable frustrations. Again, the imagination is crucial.

Conformist, repressed, neurotic, the wave-of-the-future couple, Nick and Honey, lack the passionate energy that would enable them to control their own fates. Like their lives, their marriage has been "taken for granted." Unfortunately, Nick is bright, a biologist who experiments with chromosomes in the hope of creating human types to order—an intention that troubles humanist George. This expert in the routine of an impersonal science is lost in Martha and George's highly fantasized world. Since Nick and Honey base their lives on unexamined illusions, George is able in no time to reduce their marriage to obscene dust, remarking, "I hate hypocrisy."

George took up talk after he allowed Martha's father to block publication of his first novel. Martha and George are very good indeed in their repartée; like *commedia dell'arte* zanies, they repeatedly enact scenes. George is the more devastatingly inventive, but Martha, once off and running, is the more swinishly effective. She achieves barbarisms that aesthetic George must deftly avoid. Yet George plays the game of withering insult with all his being, for imagination is all he has, while Martha regards the combat as a mere escape-valve for emotions firmly rooted in her consumer mentality. This difference becomes clear in the scene where Martha encourages Nick to "hump the hostess." At first she gives George numerous chances to stop her—any sign of compassion or generosity would do it. Why does George prefer to turn to a book? Given his immense stake in the values of lucidity and imagination, he cannot do otherwise: despite the anguish of the moment, George delights in the image of himself reading while Martha sweats in bed upstairs, for this symbolic revelation of their distinct modes of fleeing the world is too splendid!

After Martha's attempted infidelity, George, who had left the house, re-enters with a bunch of snapdragons which he hurls like spears at Martha and Nick: small phalli of his graceful symbolic revenge. In this one scene, George's commitment to imaginary deeds is completely visible. Martha pleads that the adultery didn't really come off, but George keeps hurling the snapdragons. She cries, "Truth or illusion, George. Doesn't it matter to you?" And George hurls another stalk. The truth for Martha is in the act. For George, intention is the truth.

Thus we come to the question of whether the invented child is an artistic error. Since George (and, to a lesser extent, Martha) is both motivated and gifted enough to sustain that myth, my answer is obvious. Sterile in so many ways, they cannot live with their sterility. With the child, George achieves—if only in fantasy—his crazy wish to perpetuate history "in spite of history" and to keep it under his control a little longer. The fantasy-baby gives Martha someone all her own, to use any way she wants, just as countless women have used their actual children. The motives are not extraordinary, although the resources George brings to the project and his final exorcism of the fantasy are.

At the Masque Theatre in New York, shortly after the play opened, Albee was asked what he thought of O'Neill's message in *The Iceman Cometh* that life-illusions are necessary. He replied that he felt O'Neill had made a very strong case, but that perhaps in the long run it was best for people to try to live with the truth.

The tension between truth and illusion is at the heart of Albee's plays. That so many critics condemned the invented child is a comment on the American tendency to respect only the pragmatic and down-to-earth, and to distrust the abstract and intangible. This is the audience's problem, not Albee's—he is entitled to any aesthetic means that work, and this "device" of the child works. However, Albee has been acutely aware of his problems in communicating; his response has been to allow directors, chiefly Alan Schneider, to stress the matter-of-fact possibilities in the scripts, keeping the Broadway customers from confronting the full asthetic, moral, and intellectual difficulties. But there are side-effects, among them the loss of perspective in which the more audacious "devices" could be understood.

. . . Tiny Alice

Tiny Alice again shows a character's sustained effort to live by imagined values. However, this is the first Albee play in which the form of symbolic transcendence is *expressed from within*. Everything said and enacted—erotic and ascetic, matter-of-fact and fantastic, incisive and elusive—is Brother Julian's revery.

This is not immediately apparent. The first scene is a struggle over Julian's fate between the forces of humane concern and material temptation; the fight is rigged, as the Cardinal is scarcely more humane than his tempters, Miss Alice and her Lawyer. Offered $100 million a year for twenty years in return for sending Julian— apparently once his lover—to Miss Alice, the Cardinal hardly hesitates. His Church career dominates him even when the pistol is finally raised to kill Julian. As for the Lawyer, the Cardinal is right to describe him as a hyena who tears open at the anus the carrion it finds along the trail of the real predators. (I might add that writers from Freud on have discussed anality as the basis of the capitalist ethos.)

The battle between the Cardinal and the Lawyer is lively but unfair, because whatever its basis in real events it is now occurring in Julian's mind, and is rehearsed only to show cause for Julian's drive toward martyrdom. Critics have generally liked this opening section, but they have failed to grasp the play's development. *Tiny Alice* has the logic peculiar to sexual revery; it is compulsive, ambiguous, and obsessive in its events as well as in its language. As Julian tremulously nears the subjective and fantasized heart of his experience, the semblance of rational causation fades. The revery accompanies orgasm or is its sublimated counterpart. We cannot guess this at first. But as the morning sunlight fades into the dark recesses of spirit and the senses the imagery begins to equivocate between gross sensuality and soaring asceticism, and we begin to understand. Then all light vanishes; the "mouse in the model" on stage—an emblematic Julian—dies. The breath and heartbeat of Julian, or whoever is imagining all this, resound to every corner of the theater—this is how we hear our own vital organs when relaxing into sleep or, I suppose, death.

In the initial clarity the males included the Lawyer, a hated father-figure who has been Mommy's lover and now schemes to do the dreamer harm, and the Cardinal, who was the beloved but has succumbed to the despicable values of the father-figure. Enter Mommy as the world's most powerful woman. At first she seems a dreadful hag, but soon she becomes seductive. These exhilarating and terrifying changes correspond to a rising flood of emotion recollected, and not in tranquility. Sexual memories and hallucinations pour forth as the language fragments toward grandiose symbolism or erotic caress. A stable groom with hair-tufts on his thumbs; much talk of hair on muscled men's backs; images of penetration by a gladiator's thumbs, by a lion's claws, by the Holy Spirit, all haunt Julian. He recounts the speech of the woman in the asylum who implored the divinity to enter her, a speech climaxed by her verbal "ejaculation" (says Julian), after which all subsided into nothingness. The microcosm of the play's form is in that speech. In turn, a climax to Julian's revery—his ejaculation—comes when the Lawyer fires into the dreamer's abdomen, and the martyr collapses as "blood" spreads over his groin. The other figures, now unimportant, leave. The saint is alone with his pain and ecstasy; his organs throb; the imagining reaches its epiphany.

This is symbolic transcendence with a vengeance. But, although it is grounded in masturbatory fantasy, the play makes powerful statements about the nature of that transcendence and the world which induces some to attempt it. Essentially, *Tiny Alice* asserts no values other than those men create. Life is "chance," which men edit into "mystery," the purposes they create for themselves. The Cardinal urges Julian to "accept what you do not understand." "We do not know anything," but a man can develop his "special priesthood" although "an act of faith is required." It is better to "accept" a course leading to saintliness than, like the Cardinal and the Lawyer, to become symbol rather than symbolic transcender.

We all are "instruments" whose value, though self-chosen, is conferred from without; it is best to elude the trappings of material power and to answer "How will I know thee, Oh Lord?" with "By my faith!" For, as Julian says, "My faith and my sanity—they are one and the same." All of us are waiting "until the pelvic cancer comes." But to follow one's individual idea of meaningful existence, "not losing God's light, but joining it to my own," is the secret of "how to come out on top, going under." Since "consciousness is pain" and all go under, says Albee, why not at least shape your own path? And he gives us Julian.

We are in the land of a strange metaphysics, communicated through "mental sex play" and with the godhead a woman who becomes, for the pilgrim martyr, anything he requires her to be. Thus Alice is actually "something very small enclosed in something else" (Albee to *Newsweek*). That "else" is at first her institutional wealth. Then, as Julian moves toward saintliness, Alice becomes the Bride of Christ. As he dies, she cradles him in her arms, deliberately in the pose of Michelangelo's Pietà. Julian has created her, first as his nemesis, haunting him with childhood terrors; then, in his triumphant apostate, she becomes Elysium.

Supporting Julian's web of associations is a neo-Platonic "philosophy" of appearance and substance which Albee takes as a metaphor of symbol and substance in social and aesthetic life. Made concrete on stage in the model of the mansion with its mysterious reflection of outside events, this static system intellectualizes and extrudes what is—and should have remained—implicit in Albee's art. Yet it is not hard to see why Albee wished to elaborate it. His plays are allegories saying "this is the *essence* of how it is"; that is the function of his family. The Cardinal provides a good example of what this method does and does not achieve. In the Masque Theatre discussion, Albee talked about Brecht's *Galileo*, which he had seen at the Berliner Ensemble. The scene of the Cardinal-turned-Pope being dressed while the Inquisitor keeps at him for permission to show Galileo the torture instruments had particularly impressed Albee. The meaning of the Brecht scene, however, is in its process: as more and more garments of the Papal authority are placed over his shoulders, and as the footsteps of the faithful continue without cease, the man's consciousness of his obligations to an office and situation becomes overpowering. In contrast, Albee's Cardinal is never capable of choice; allegory rather than process unfolds; the Cardinal merely does what Albee *a priori* deems necessary to his office; and where Brecht had shown a specific opportunity for a knowing man to exercise a social function with more or less rigidity or humanity, Albee builds a metaphysic while denying man freedom within a social role. *Tiny Alice* offers one of the purest recent embodiments of the enticing notion that man is born free and enchained by society. No wonder Albee has difficulty showing the dynamics of men within their institutions, and tends to come up with marginal aesthetic "notes," to the damage of his art.

Findings

Albee the satirist is without peer among American playwrights as he crisply negates destructive values through the medium of his family. His ability to affirm values, however, is limited by unconscious acceptance of some attitudes of that very consensus he scorns in other respects, and by the family structure he uses so well for scorn. He also is too close to his heroes, so that when he goes beyond satire his language thickens into solemn rhetoric. At the crucial moments—to return to the problems with which I began this essay—Albee is neither untruthful nor unskillful. But taking the plays in their entirety, what Albee despises provides yeast for his drama; what he hopes is too often chaff.

The basis of Albee's affirmation is stated by George, speaking to Nick: "You disgust me on principle, and you're a smug son of a bitch personally, but I'm trying to give you a survival kit. DO YOU HEAR ME?" Nick replies, "UP YOURS!" and George continues:

> You take the trouble to construct a civilization . . . to . . . to build a society, based on the principles of . . . of principle . . . you endeavor to make communicable sense out of natural order, morality out of the unnatural disorder of man's mind . . . you make government and art, and realize that they are, must be, both the same . . . you bring things to the saddest of all points . . . to the point where there *is* something to lose . . . then all at once, through all the music, through all the sensible sounds of men building, attempting, comes the *Dies Irae*. And what is it? What does the trumpet sound? Up yours. I suppose there's justice to it, after all the years . . . Up yours.

The playwright's grimace and defensive wit fall away; the wicked sybarite is uttering a Liberal's cautions. Government is a form of art and art a means of government. The world goes around because of work, principle, morality.

This world is threatened by the moral vacuity of the Nicks and —what? As George refills Nick's glass he tells us:

> Here we are . . . ice for the lamps of China, Manchuria thrown in. *To Nick.* You better watch those yellow bastards, my love . . . they aren't amused. Why don't you come over to our side, and we'll blow the hell out of 'em. Then we can split up the money between us and be on easy street. What d'ya say?

George, though sarcastic, is quite serious. The West has somehow allowed the Chinese to grow militant as it goes slack, and resistance to the "yellow bastards" is in order. Their threatening independence might be put down if America could recoup purpose and unity, and overseas wealth would pour in as before.

The meaning of the passage is unequivocal, and casts new light on Albee's championing of pioneer attitudes. Apparently he also favors the Liberal principle of building America by exploiting other peoples: Spanish, French, Mexicans, and above all the Negro and the Indian. George's speech bristles with ugly fear in the face of change. Nor is George alone in expressing this hostility to the aspirations of others. The Nurse in *The Death of Bessie Smith* also resists such change—again, her speech is not in an ironical context which would "criticize" it, as was her "sick of civilization" speech cited earlier, for example—when she envisions with a shudder a Negro "millennium" and "a great black mob marching down the street, banners in the air." *Tiny Alice* has nothing but cliché cynicisms to offer on the topic of radical social change. "Every dictator was once a colonel who vowed to retire, once the revolution was over" and "it is easy to postpone elections." Alice even gives money to some revolutions, along with churches, symphonies, and other reliable institutions. One wonders how the example of the American revolution can have been lost on such "thinking," unless the cause be present-day chauvinism. Yet Albee's terror of other people's rebellious autonomy is of a piece with the American Liberal outlook; now, especially, it blinds one to the agencies of historical affirmation. Thus George:

> When people can't abide things as they are, when they can't abide the present, they do one of two things . . . either they turn to a contemplation of the past, as I have done, or they set about to . . . to alter the future.

His distaste for the latter direction is expressed in a phrase drawn from Martha's sexual conduct: "When you want to change something . . . you BANG! BANG! BANG!"

Left as he is without acceptable doorways to the future, Albee inevitably must end his American family in sterility. This limits his range as a dramatist. "The discord between the present and the past," as Chekhov said, "is first of all felt in the family," yet if one's imagery *ends* there, without exploring the worlds of play, struggle, and work, human potential scarcely can be known. Albee has depicted a hospital, a beach, a Cardinal's residence, yet family relations remain paramount for each. If the plays are to be believed, history will end in the aestheticism of symbolic transcendence. History will continue, of course, and will say something about the limits of Albee's dramatic vision.

Drama is the most socially rooted of the arts, and aestheticism as an affirmation has never been wholly comfortable on stage. Because Albee is so incapable of *historical* affirmations, he identifies too closely with his symbolic transcenders and loses aesthetic distance. These difficulties become audible in George's rhetoric when he is serious: the spark of slang goes and his speech becomes amazingly opaque. This is even more true in *Tiny Alice,* since all the characters' language is projected in Julian's mind and can be turned into dry cant. Tired, unfelt commonplaces about the Human Condition abound, ritually uttered substitutes for real human conditions enacted in history.

In *Tiny Alice* a final problem also comes to a head, caused by Albee's uncritical presentation of his heroes. Julian's imagination, which creates the action, is too homosexual for general application or comprehension. Most plays "compromise universality" in the other direction; they generalize and fantasize about existence with an implicit heterosexuality just as narrow, and just as blandly disregard the other side of sexuality. However, though a homosexual viewpoint may make some special contribution, it is less generally valid, balanced, and embracing than is the best pondered heterosexual outlook, given a world in which the homosexual still is despised and persecuted. It may be intensively and effectively expressed—Genet's *Our Lady of the Flowers,* as well as *Tiny Alice,* shows what remarkable art is thus engendered. But as a rule art gains when a writer pleads neither the homosexual nor the heterosexual vision, but maintains a nice understanding and irony for both. The homosexual vision is not in itself debilitating; what hurts is not to have it set in the broadest perspective.

What's the Matter with Edward Albee?

by Tom F. Driver

The nation's publicity media, desperately in search of a "gifted young playwright," and unable to practice that asceticism of taste which is the requisite of culture, have praised the mediocre work of Edward Albee as if it were excellence. They have made the author of six bad plays into a man of fame and fortune, which is his good luck. They have also made him into a cultural hero, which is not good for anybody. It is time to disentangle our judgments of his merits from the phenomenon of his popularity.

Four of Edward Albee's six bad plays are too short to fill an evening. Another is a dead adaptation of a famous story. The sixth is the most pretentious American play since *Mourning Becomes Electra*. In each of these works there are serious, even damning, faults obvious to anyone not predisposed to overlook them. To get Albee in perspective, we should examine first the faults and then the predisposition of the audience not to see them. As a maker of plots, Albee hardly exists. Both *The Zoo Story*, his first play performed in New York and *Who's Afraid of Virginia Woolf?*, his most successful, are built upon an unbelievable situation—namely, that a sane, average-type person would be a passive spectator in the presence of behavior obviously headed toward destructive violence. In *The Zoo Story*, why does Peter just sit there while Jerry works himself up to suicide? Why doesn't Nick, in *Who's Afraid?*, take his young wife and go home when he sees that George and Martha want only to fight the whole night through? In both cases, the answer is either that there is some psychological explanation that has not been written into the play, or that if Peter or Nick did the logical thing and went home the play would be over.

Sometimes it is argued that this objection is out of place. It is

"What's the matter with Edward Albee?" by Tom F. Driver. From *The Reporter* (January 2, 1964). © 1964 by The Reporter Magazine Company. Reprinted by permission of the author and his agent, James Brown Associates, Inc.

69452

held that the passivity of Peter and Nick is allegorical and is supposed to point to our general passivity in the presence of destructive tendencies in modern life. But this is cheap allegory. A situation cannot function well as allegory unless it is a believable situation. Whatever allegorical element is present in the situation of *The Zoo Story* and *Who's Afraid?* is in conflict with the realistic convention that both plays assume.

Failure to maintain the chosen convention occurs in all the Albee plays, even in *The American Dream,* which does not pretend to realism but is more like the "theater of the absurd." It opens in such a manner as to suggest that Albee is imitating Ionesco, or perhaps will parody him. After ten minutes it is no longer clear whether any reference to Ionesco is intended, and it never becomes clear in the rest of the play. On the other hand, no different convention imposes itself. Toward the end of the play the comic mode is destroyed by a long autobiographical speech by the title character, a speech so full of Freudian cliché and self-pity that the only humane response to it is to be embarrassed for the author. No one could have written it who did not regard himself above his art. In the work of amateurs we expect this sort of thing, we forgive it. But we do not praise it, for to do so is to substitute indulgence for criticism.

Who's Afraid? displays another failure to maintain convention. This play is supposedly a realistic depiction of "how life is." I have yet to hear a reasoned defense of it on any other grounds, including that of its director, Alan Schneider (*Tulane Drama Review,* Spring 1963). Yet we are shown a married couple who go through life as the "parents" of a twenty-one-year-old "son" who is purely imaginary. The play ends when this "son" is sent to an imaginary "death" by his "father."

To be sure, the message of *Who's Afraid?* is clear in spite of this confusion; too clear. In many marriages illusions grow and have to be "exorcised" (this pretentious, crypto-religious word is Albee's), in order to save what is left of the partners. But the device Albee uses to state such a truism is once again from Ionesco. Patched into a realistic play, it turns the whole into a crazy mixture of the obvious and the incredible. This is not, as some have said, a problem in the third act only. The flaw that ruins the third act is already present in the first two, rendering them unbelievable.

Patching and stitching is the mark of Albee's style, if bad habits may be called a style. Scarcely five lines go by without making one feel that something extraneous has been sewn in. The scenes have no rhythm. They give no impression of having developed organically from situations deeply felt or from ideas clearly perceived. Nothing is followed through in the terms initially proposed. There is no obedience to reality outside the playwright's head, nor much evidence of consistency within it.

If Albee's arbitrary manner puts an unnecessary and uninstructive burden upon the audience, it also gives the actors more to do than they can accomplish. The exhaustion that the actors, as well as the audience, say they feel at the end of *Who's Afraid?* does not come from having experienced too much but from having pretended to experience it. All acting involves pretense, but there is such a thing as being supported by a role. Albee's roles have to be supported by the actors.

The performances of Uta Hagen and Arthur Hill in *Who's Afraid?* are remarkable to see, yet they are pathetic. These two skillful people are forced to manufacture on stage, moment by moment, semblances of character which the script not only does not support but even undercuts. The more brilliantly they perform, the more anguish we feel. But it is anguish for the performers. Arthur Hill manages his tour de force by holding desperately all evening to a few mannerisms, such as his gait, the unbalanced carriage of his shoulders, and his operatic delivery of the lines. Uta Hagen, with more variety, pulls even more tricks out of her professional trunk. In the course of the play's three and a half hours, it is the actors rather than the characters who become hysterical. Faced with the same hurdle in *The Ballad of the Sad Café,* Colleen Dewhurst takes a more dignified recourse. Given no intelligible character to enact, she refuses to pretend to act. She poses. Hers is the most beautiful example of non-acting I have ever seen, and I applaud her for it. No slightest hint of emotion escapes to betray the purity of her refusal; she is on strike, declining to do the playwright's work for him.

The falseness of Albee's characters is also due to the fact that they are but surrogates for more authentic ones. The characters who could make psychological sense of *Who's Afraid?* are not the two couples on stage but the four homosexuals for whom they are standing in. Granted that George is not very masculine and Martha not feminine, still we are asked to accept them as a heterosexual couple who might love each other. Their mutual sado-masochism renders this request absurd. They maintain their fight with increased pleasure-pain all night long.

I do not deny that heterosexual couples engage in *some* of the

same behavior and show *some* of the same psychology. They do.
But a play built around such an orgy invites us to ask what part
of life it most aptly refers to. The answer is not to marriages but
to homosexual liaisons. The play hides from the audience its real
subject. This is quite apart from the question whether Albee *knows*
what the real subject is. I think he does, but if not his job as a playwright is to find out. And to make his play tell it. We are driven to
saying that either Albee does not know what he is saying or else that
he is afraid to say what he means.

The significant cultural fact we have to deal with is not the existence of Albee's six bad plays but the phenomenon of their popularity. The public has been sold a bill of goods, but there must be
reasons why it is willing to buy. What are these reasons?

Whatever may be said against Albee—and I've only said the
half of it—one must also say that his bent is wholly theatrical. All
his mistakes are theatrical mistakes. He confuses theatrical conventions, but he does not, except in *The Ballad of the Sad Café*, confuse the genre of playwriting with that of film, novel, or television.
This is rare in today's theater. I expect this instinct for the theatrical
is what people really have in mind when they refer to Albee's talent.
"Talent" is the wrong word, for the nature of a talent is to grow,
and Albee shows no signs of that. He does show a theatrical instinct.

Although theatricality is an important component in all great
drama, it can also characterize some of the worst. That is, it can
be used imaginatively or it can be used merely fancifully. Albee's
use is the latter. There is evidence that this is a direct cause of his
success. The truly imaginative use of theatricality is found today
in Samuel Beckett, Eugène Ionesco, and Jean Genet, none of whom
has ever caught on with the large New York theater audience. Critics
on the daily papers either misinterpret these playwrights (the *New
York Times* told us recently that Genêt's *The Maids* is a "social
tract") or they find them "obscure." Albee is preferred not because
he is better but because he is worse. Since his themes are obvious,
even hackneyed, they cannot be obscure. And his reckless inventiveness can pass for complexity without forcing anyone to entertain a
complex thought. In short, he provides a theatrical effect conveniently devoid of imaginative substance.

This accounts, I believe, for the so-called "involvement" of the
audience at *Who's Afraid of Virginia Woolf?* Since the situation and
the characters are false, the play provides an occasion for the display of pseudo-emotions: mock anger, mock hatred, mock envy, and
finally mock love. These are provided on stage by the actors, with

whom the audience enters into complicity. Thus the audience achieves, at no expense to its real emotions, a mock catharsis.

In addition, there is reason to suppose that the very roughness and the gaucheries that mar Albee's plays contribute to his success. Most of the values that operate in our society are drawn from the bourgeois ideal of domestic harmony, necessary for the smooth functioning of the machine. Yet we know that there are subconscious desires fundamentally in conflict with the harmonious ideal. Albee satisfies at once the ideal and the hidden protest against it. In his badly written plays he jabs away at life with blunt instruments. If his jabbing hit the mark, that would be another matter. But it doesn't, no more than does the child in the nursery when he tears up his toys. That is why Albee is the pet of the audience, this little man who looks as if he dreamed of evil but is actually mild as a dove and wants to be loved. In him America has found its very own playwright. He's a dream.

Broadway

by Francis Fergusson

The entertainment industry is, of course, not confined to this country. Our plays and films are exported all over the world, and now Europe, and even Japan, contribute their share to the flood of mass entertainment. What makes Broadway unique is that it represents not only commercial entertainment but also *the* theater: in this country no other conception of the theater—of its possible value or meaning, its place in society, or its role in the life of our culture—has ever taken root. Thus we look to Broadway to provide our equivalent of Sophocles and Molière, and at the same time judge it (along with the night clubs) as a going concern in the "luxury" field.

Everyone knows Broadway, where it glitters, with a more snobbish and expensive glitter, among the movie palaces, flea circuses, and dance halls of midtown Manhattan. It is a part of our folklore, like football weekends and political rallies. Moreover, the structure of Broadway as a business, and the conditions it imposes on its artists, have often been explained. Not much that is new remains to be said about Broadway, but perhaps it is appropriate to assemble the picture again. For Broadway is the most constant element in our theater's life—the "normal" place of that art with us.

The excitement which we associate with Broadway comes less from the shows we see there than from the heady gamble of *producing* a show. The odds are all against the producer; as business, Broadway is riskier than gold bricks or swamplands in Florida. No one knows, in advance, whether a show will be a hit; but everyone knows that the initial costs and the running costs are so high that unless it *is* a hit everyone will lose a great deal of money, and, what is more dangerous, the reputation of marketability (in the case of

"Broadway" by Francis Fergusson. From *The Human Image in Dramatic Literature* (New York: Doubleday Anchor Books, 1957). © 1957 by Francis Fergusson and reprinted with his permission.

the artists) and of being able to guess the market (in the case of the producer). But when a show is a hit the national slot machine suddenly pours forth its flood of gold, and all who have been connected with the show are instantly promoted to the status of "luminous," "compassionate," and "incandescent" artists of the theater.

This game seems to satisfy the gamblers' instincts of the angels and producers, and the more guileless appetite for glamour of the Broadway audience; but the cold-eyed interests that control Broadway do not share in any of the excitement. Those who can count on making money are the owners of Broadway real estate; the unions of stagehands, electricians, scene painters, costume makers, truckers, and box-office attendants; and auxiliary professionals like the press agents and the play reviewers on the big dailies. These elements all enjoy monopolies in their various realms, and are thus in a position to exact their "take" from every show in advance. It is they who make the risk of production so absurdly high; but they do not themselves take any risk; they leave that to the producers and their angels, and to the artists who actually work on the show. It is a system which guarantees the stability of the monopolistic business and labor interests surrounding Broadway, and the complete instability of anything which could be called "theater."

Though nothing in the show shops lasts, a certain fairly constant atmosphere is generated—recognizable but indefinable; the pretentious but somewhat guilty atmosphere of show-business-as-theater: the curious essence we know as Broadway. Whatever appears on Times Square has some of this Broadway look, as though the neighborhood itself could confer it, like those infallible acids whereby Hollywood can bleach any young girl, however charming she may be herself, into this year's standard starlet. Sartre's play, *Les Mains Sales,* is one thing in the French film, quite another as the Broadway play, *Red Gloves.* The actor who seems quite at home in one of the big money-makers on Times Square may be quite different, two months later, when he sneaks off to play in the Village. Some of the same individuals who constituted the exciting audiences for the Federal Theatre now make up that totally different thing, a Broadway audience. I think, therefore, that the Broadway atmosphere is not due to those who work there, but rather to the stereotyped postures which the show-shop regime forces upon them. If we can't define the mind and taste of Broadway, we may be able to understand something about it by remembering how its producers and its artists are obliged to work.

The producer is a key figure in the Broadway setup. Anyone who has, or can find, the money can be a producer; but those who last in this profession for a few years are obliged to develop the special caginess, the impersonal craftiness, of the market diagnostician. In this job there is very little room for the exercise of personal taste, and the producer renounces that luxury early in his career, unless he happens to be a natural thermometer of the entertainment market, like the fabulous hero of *Once in a Lifetime*. As entrepreneur, he is between the investor (or angel) and the show. But he cannot afford his own acting company, theater, director, designer, or musician; his own organization consists of a small office and a skeleton office staff. He shops around for stars with "names," directors and designers with good reputations, orchestrators who have, as nearly as may be, the infallible touch; and out of these elements (often quite strange to each other) he puts together his show. The arts of the producer are thus essentially those of merchandising, and the producer is very much like the buyer in a big department store, or the designer of shopwindows. In New York, the world's richest city, he commands the same resources as the fashion experts and the decorators of Persian night clubs and Tudor tearooms. Hence the sleek, expensive, tasteless quality of the typical Broadway success. Everything in it has cost a lot of money, and can subdue the meek herds of patrons with the authority of the market itself.

It is those who actually make the show—directors, actors, designers, and the rest—who occupy the most false and impossible position in this system. There are no permanent jobs for them on Broadway, and of course no possibility of learning how to work together, or of developing their own art and their own taste. They are strictly marketable commodities in a buyers' market; no wonder they lose their human flavor so soon, looking less and less like themselves, and more and more like the ads for whiskey, perfume, and Caribbean cruises.

We sometimes tend to think that it is the professional playwrights who make Broadway what it is. But if they are to play the game of the entertainment market, they must accept its subtle rules like everyone else: they too must consult the market first, and their own taste and intelligence second. This point was explained with impressive clarity by Mr. Abe Burrows in a recent issue of *The New York Times'* Sunday Theatre Page. "Playwrights," he says,

> are the products of their culture. They reflect every strength and weakness of the culture, both as artists and as human beings. This is a confused age we live in and the dramas depicting it are bound to be just as confused. This is an age that equates value with success.

In fact, it values only success and, in turn, success is largely measured in terms of money. In striving for this monetary success, all of us are scrambling in a huge market place. Our playwrights are right smack in the middle of that market place, too. And that is a deadly spot for a man who is trying to give some insight into his world.

It is the critics on the daily papers who render the first verdict of failure or "success." For this reason the daily-reviewer is more feared and cursed one minute, and worshiped with more tearful gratitude the next, than anything on Broadway except the box office itself. But it is, I think, as unrealistic to blame the (often good-hearted) individual reviewers as it is to blame the playwrights. The job itself of daily-reviewing is an integral part of the Broadway system, and as such is surrounded with so many subtle taboos that the occupant of the job has little chance to develop an intelligible point of view of his own. The critics on the weeklies are much freer to consult their own taste; it is to them that we must look for "criticism" in the usual sense of the word.

The job of daily-reviewer is firmly based on the mystery of Broadway itself: the paradox of show business as theater. Thus, the reviewer in his aisle seat represents the hoped-for customer, like the buyer at a fashion show. He is called upon to exercise some choice among the products hopefully displayed; but he knows that his reputation as market diagnostician is at stake—that the excellent trade journal *Variety* will publish, in the spring, an analysis of the reports of the daily-reviewers, grading them according to their ability to pick a hit. He also knows that, as part of the entertainment industry, he must do his share to "create" a market. This requirement is clearly suggested in the following rather rueful paragraph by Mr. Walter Kerr . . . in *How Not to Write a Play:*

> For one reason or another, the contemporary American cannot be persuaded that the legitimate drama is a tolerable form of entertainment. All sorts of persuasions are repeatedly tried. The newspaper reviewers, for instance, flirt with perjury in the nightly effort to make the theater seem gay. One recent Broadway season was, by common consent, the worst in the memory of man. The plays which went to make up this season were described in the daily press as "stunning," "magnificent," "exuberant," "distinguished," "exhilarating," "enormously enjoyable," "enchanting," "extraordinary," and "filled with wit, talent and splendor." The playgoer remained skeptical.

The daily-reviewer is thus necessarily part of show *business;* but as guardian of the Broadway mystery he must write his verdicts (in about half an hour, around midnight the day the show opens) with the mysterious air of the connoisseur of the arts of the theater. It is perhaps for that reason that he finds such adjectives as Mr. Kerr quotes—encomiums which would make Shakespeare blush—for the lucky show that meets with his approval. And when a play rubs him the wrong way, whether it be by Lorca, Cummings, or Dostoevski, or the stage-struck wife of one of the angels, he damns it utterly, as though he spoke for the theater in general—or as though his sense of the Broadway market gave him the authority to decide whether any play was "theater" at all.

Mr. Kerr's remarks suggest that the daily-reviewers cannot create a hit. For a show to be a hit—i.e., make money—it must run for two months, or, if it is a big musical, for eight or ten months at least; and no form of promotion can guarantee that. But the reviewers do have the power to kill a show, because most theatergoers look at their reports when deciding where to go. There are few if any instances of a show which has survived the disapproval of the daily-reviewers, even when enthusiastically supported by the producer, the critics on the weeklies, and interested members of the audience. The daily-reviewer is thus an important part of the mechanism whereby the Broadway taste or atmosphere is maintained: he can exile to outer darkness the many kinds of theater which are not "Broadway."

Mr. Burrows, in the article from which I have quoted, suggests some of the reasons why we look to "success measured largely in terms of money" to decide all questions of value. Our age, as he says, is confused; which means, I take it, that we do not know what forms of life or art to choose. As individuals we may be guided by habits, tastes, and ideas derived from our own experience, and from the particular regional or racial or religious tradition in which we were brought up. But in public we do not express this taste. We know that all traditions lose most of their meaning in the national scene, and that the little-understood forces of our industrial society are changing the scene with increasing speed. It is natural, at this bewildered moment, to let the market rule, for its pronouncements are as impersonal and as mathematically accurate as those of a Geiger counter. And they carry great authority; for unless a man can "meet a market" he may fail, undernourished both physically and spiritually, while meeting a market may bring fabulous wealth. The market seems to know what forms of life and art are destined to survive in our society. It is easier to trust it—out of timidity, respect for money, and hopeful good will—than to attempt moral or esthetic judgments of one's own.

It is, of course, the media of mass entertainment and mass advertising which present the human image with the widest public acceptance. Those who confect the shows, the commercials, and the advertisements which absorb millions of listeners, viewers, and magazine readers twenty-four hours a day appear to follow the principle expressed by Sabina in Mr. Thornton Wilder's *The Skin of Our Teeth*: "I don't think the theater is a place where people's feelings ought to be hurt," she says. Her sentiment is friendly; it is easy to recognize in it our inarticulate need for some cozy realm of the spirit where we might all be the same nice people together. Our faith in the market is sustained by a flabby version of our faith in democracy itself, and the taboos which surround the mass media, ruling out all reference to differences among us, whether regional or racial or religious, or even of age—for all grandmothers are as spry as maidens by this rule, as they sprint out to the backyard to hang up the wash, or pull a pie from the oven with an inanely brilliant grin—reveal perhaps, not only our techniques for seducing the consumer, but an element of tender democratic delicacy. But the mass media, when thus strictly limited, are impervious to most of the actualities of human life: they make that "non-conducting atmosphere" which Henry James mentioned. Backed by the authority of our gravest industrialists, the weight of vast wealth, and the magic of applied science, the image of *Homo Americanus* which flickers on a million screens and is murmured simultaneously into a million ears is of unbearable silliness, like the childishness of senility.

As market, Broadway belongs in the comparatively small "luxury" class, and the vision of human life which it projects is more like that of the "after-shave club" than that of the ads, in family magazines, for trusses or detergents. Its initial appeal is snobbish—to those who can afford it. But the ideal of universal marketability exercises a strong and ever-increasing pressure upon it. Hollywood began as a distended suburb of Broadway, but now it would be truer to say that Broadway is an uneasy and less and less important suburb of Hollywood, radio, and TV. Arrangements for movie and TV rights become the most important part of a Broadway contract, and without the golden hope of the mass market, the afterlife in the mass media, it is doubtful whether Broadway would continue to exist.

I have been endeavoring to describe the general situation of Broadway, and the key figures in the show-shop regime: the producer, the performers, the playwright, and the daily-reviewer, as a way of understanding the flickering life on Times Square: the docility of the paying customer; the falsity which the market regime forces upon even the finest professionals; the artificially hopped-up excitement which accompanies a hit, the irrational violence with which a show felt to be "not Broadway" is rejected. But the basic paradox of Broadway is that it is not only a show *shop,* but also all we normally have as a theater; and this paradox accounts, I think, both for the frustrations of Broadway artists and for the fact that a more vital kind of theater from time to time crashes through there. The best foreign companies are marketed on Broadway; now and then a production which has succeeded in London will be imported, and work, for a time, as a *succès d'estime.* And every now and then a new artist, performer or playwright who is a "natural," will be put over by a shrewd agent. Our theater artists are obliged to besiege Broadway, and the market itself (as it speaks in box-office figures, "success measure in money") is impartial: it cannot distinguish between a living and a dead piece of theater, but only between one that makes money and one that does not. And it is these unpredictable signs of life which lead some lovers of the theater to hope that Broadway itself will change, turning at length from a show shop into a real theater.

But these hopes have been expressed regularly for thirty or forty years, and Broadway is still Broadway, much as it was in the twenties. Foreign companies come and go, but they have little visible effect on what we do, or upon the mind and taste of the daily-reviewers. New artists appear, but even the best of them seem to have less effect on the Broadway regime than it does on them. I tried to suggest how this works in my remarks on the history of our theater between the wars.

The fact is that Broadway, its structure, and its habits of mind and feeling are firmly rooted in our market-ruled society. I do not see how our "theater" can ever be more than this small and extremely precarious luxury market, unless some common vision of human nature and destiny appears among us. In the meantime the notion of theater-as-show-shop expresses a deep if unadmitted feeling, on everyone's part, that our theater has as yet little of general interest or value to show.

Off-Broadway:
Editor's Note

At this point in this collection, an article should appear on the Off-Broadway theater to provide a bridge between Broadway, on one hand, and the strange theatrical worlds beyond, where "Happenings" occur and the theatrical impulse, freed from all preconceptions and traditions, takes any shape the imagination dictates. Articles on the Off-Broadway theater, however, take one of two turns, neither of which is suitable for this collection. Either they quickly become chronologies, enumerating the many theater groups that formed shortly after World War II, flourished in the "golden age" of Off-Broadway in the late 1950s, and declined into the financial disaster of the 1960s; or they turn at once to detailing the sad economic facts of New York theatrical production that have destroyed the talent and idealism poured into the little theaters. As an excellent and useful example of the chronological approach, I suggest Chapter 10, "Off-Broadway," of Gerald Weales' *American Drama Since World War II*; and as a clear, forceful statement of the "dollars-and-drama" approach, no better discussion can be found than the interview between Off-Broadway producer Judith Marechal and Charles L. Mee, Jr., in the Fall, 1965 issue of *Tulane Drama Review*.

Off-Broadway has never represented, it seems obvious now, any fundamental challenge to Broadway, never questioned the basic Broadway assumptions about the nature of theater—as the later, more radical theaters have. Instead, Off-Broadway has tried to put back into the conventional theater those crucial elements missing from the Broadway patterns: theatrical taste, honesty in subject matter and technique, a willingness to experiment with new plays and different styles. But Broadway has always paid lip service to these values, and so it became no great trick to move an Off-Broadway show to Broadway, or to reverse the direction. Similarly, actors and directors trained Off-Broadway found it possible to move from there to the brighter lights of Broadway or Hollywood without any violent wrench of their artistic attitudes.

Some critics have cynically suggested that Off-Broadway has always been no more than the minor leagues, a group of farm teams, where all the players are merely waiting for a chance in the big leagues and the big money. The analogy does not hold, in my opinion, for the Off-Broadway theaters have had considerable effect on public drama in New York and in the country as a whole. They have given new playwrights—Albee and Richardson, for example—a chance to have their plays produced; they have made it acceptable to deal on the public stage, to some degree at least, with previously taboo subjects; they have shown that revivals of the classics of the theater can be effective and enjoyable; and they have developed and refined techniques in all the arts of the theater.

In short, Off-Broadway has kept Broadway at least a little alive, and it has provided the basis for many of the small city repertory companies that are beginning to spread throughout the country. But Off-Broadway itself has fallen on evil days. Judith Marechal states flatly that no Off-Broadway production now makes even enough to pay its weekly expenses, let alone repay the original investment, and she predicts that in a few years Off-Broadway theaters will house only vanity productions and the big musicals that leave Broadway in order to cut costs. This is a dreary prospect for those of us who have been able to see off Broadway a range of drama, old and new, that we never expected to find in the United States.

The Pass-the-Hat Theater Circuit

by *Elenore Lester*

"The last Off-Off-Broadway show I saw, an actress in a negligee accidentally tripped into my lap during the performance. The time before that, I got into an all-night bull session with the playwright after the show. The plays? Man, they're alive. Even when they stink, they're alive! And you get it all for a buck. Can you beat that anywhere?" The young man—pale and intense with round, steel-rimmed spectacles and longish hair—precariously tilted his wire-backed chair and balanced himself against a small, rickety table at the Cafe Cino, a cozy coffeehouse on Cornelia Street in Greenwich Village. Beside him sat his girl friend, clad like him in tight corduroy jeans and a denim work shirt. He was a painter, he said, she a "Bennington dropout." They were "OOB-niks," Off-Off-Broadway regulars, attending plays on the pass-the-hat circuit at least once a week. The two were typical of one segment of a growing audience that has discovered "underground theater" in the candle-lit coffeehouses, austere church garrets, and creaky, musty lofts of the Village and East Village. Here, for a pittance dropped into the collection box, they see original plays hot off the creative griddle by worthy but as-yet-unknown young American playwrights. In the past five years about 400 new plays and over 200 new playwrights have been introduced on the OOB circuit.

For squares who might confuse double-Off-Broadway with single-Off-Broadway, let it be known that some $19,980 and a deep artistic chasm separate the two. An Off-Broadway show must pay rent on a theater (no matter how old and tacky), hire technicians, and carry a budget to pay actors an Equity minimum. It must advertise, promote, and sell tickets. As a result, few Off-Broadway plays can hit the boards for less than $20,000. If the play is to meet expenses, it

"The Pass-the-Hat Theater Circuit" by Elenore Lester. From *The New York Times Magazine* (December 5, 1965). © 1965 by The New York Times Company and reprinted with their permission.

must appeal to critics and attract a fair-sized audience. This is why, by common consent, Off-Broadway is considered a lost cause. Rising production costs have made it unable to fulfill its original function of presenting new and experimental work without worrying about the box office. An OOB play, on the other hand, can make it on $20, and it doesn't have to please anyone but the people putting it on. In fact, it may go on before an audience of none. ("We've played it for the room," says Joe Cino of the Cornelia Street coffeehouse.) It's strictly noncommercial theater. Coffeehouses and churches supply the premises, heat and light. Nobody makes a profit. Nobody gets paid; not the actors, most of whom are thoroughly professional; not the technicians, who are skillful; not the playwrights, who are talented. Everyone is in it for love. This means that on the OOB circuit, they'll try anything if they think it's "beautiful," "interesting," "real theater," or "a challenge." Preparation for OOB plays may take one to six weeks depending on the complexity of the work, and the time available to everyone concerned. Despite limited rehearsal time, fluffs are few and far between.

What kind of productions can you put on for $20? Some very good ones indeed.

"We use warm bodies, bare boards, imagination and lots of youth and energy," says Ellen Stewart of the La Mama club (it is officially known as La Mama E.T.C.—Experimental Theater Club). This combination has given the OOB circuit a vitality that has won the attention of Edward Albee and his co-producers, Clinton Wilder and Richard Barr, who have already plucked a handful of OOB playwrights and given them Off-Broadway exposure in the Cherry Lane Theater. Many well-known painters like Larry Rivers and Andy Warhol frequent the OOB theater. It's part of the standard tour given visiting foreign literati, several of whom have said it's the most exciting theater anywhere, including Paris and Berlin, and have encouraged Miss Stewart in her recent enterprise of opening branches of La Mama E.T.C. in Paris and Copenhagen.

OOB has attracted the interest of increasing numbers of students, budding writers and artists, talent scouts, hip uptown types, and adventurous suburbanites. ("Bless those women from Scarsdale and South Orange," says playwright Robert Patrick. "They make the best audience. Nothing shocks them.") Nevertheless, the average Broadway and Off-Broadway theatergoer would not dig OOB. It is disconcerting in more ways than one. Attendance at an OOB production isn't planned months or weeks in advance. OOB audiences arrive at the "theater" at hours like 9 or 11 P.M. or 1 A.M. in attire that ranges from chic-casual to last-end beat. They usually don't know what they are going to see and no critic has told them how they are expected to respond to it. Some know the name of the play and its author from a listing in *The Village Voice,* which is the chief source of information, but they don't know much more. The *Voice* reviews only some of the plays, and often the reviews run after the play's run is over.

Even more disturbing to the conventional theatergoer than the casualness of OOB is the breakdown of the impersonality that prevails in a formal theater, where spectators sit in the dark in rows of rigid seats at a safe distance from the actors. On the OOB circuit this depersonalization is broken down by the smallness of the audience and the closeness of the actors. Members of the audience are never far enough from the stage lights to feel totally blacked out. They must, in a sense, participate in the action by keeping their chairs from grating and their coffee cups from rattling. This gives them the feeling that they count as individuals, and some OOB-niks believe this quickens their responses. They also claim that the sense of involvement and immediacy gives them a definite sensuous experience that can't be duplicated in ordinary theater, even theater-in-the-round, which still maintains a kind of formal barrier between stage action and audience response.

Part of the "sensuous experience" which might also be distasteful to the average theatergoer is the ordinary physical discomfort that is taken in stride by OOB-niks. All of the permanent OOB spots have hard chairs, but each also has its special tribulations. At the Cafe Cino, OOB audiences sit at precariously balanced tables pushed close together and risk getting coffee and actors in their laps. At the La Mama, a loft on Second Avenue near Tenth Street, they sip insipid coffee from paper cups. In the choir loft of the Judson Memorial Church on Washington Square South, a good part of the audience must take raised back seats that should be attempted only by courageous and experienced mountain climbers. At Theatre Genesis in the Church of St. Mark's in-the-Bouwerie at Second Avenue and Tenth Street, all but the early comers must contend visually with the columns that support the spare little meeting room. Audiences viewing Hardware Poets Playhouse productions now enjoy the comfort of an arena theater in the Good Shepherd-Faith Presbyterian Church on West 66th Street, but for two years they sat uncomplaining in a drafty loft above a hardware store on West 54th Street.

Obviously OOB-niks do not attend theater for a sense of afflu-ence, status, a "gala evening," the desire to find out "what everyone is talking about" or which critic was right. This audience goes to the theater to be shook up, intellectually and emotionally. Do they get shook? Often they do. Most OOB playwrights do their best to oblige. They have incorporated the techniques and outlook of the avant-garde and the Theater of the Absurd. However, the fact is that the theater of Brecht, Beckett, Genet and Ionesco represents for these young writers not the avant-garde but the traditional. OOB plays are usually short, some running no more than 35 min-utes, and usually have few characters.

Although these characters are disconnected from society, they are unlike the traditional American outcast heroes in the works of Eugene O'Neill or Tennessee Williams, who are oppressed by the hostile power of society. In this sense the young writers seem "far-ther out" than either Albee, whom they regard as an old master (a popular OOB play was *Who's Afraid of Edward Albee?*), or Le Roi Jones, author of the Off-Broadway shocker *The Toilet,* who de-spite his own youth is generally regarded as an aging bohemian somewhat tainted by commercialism. Most of the writers on the OOB circuit write as though they were born into the world the day after some metaphysical H-Bomb exploded, and they accept this blasted world as the natural environment and proceed to play around in it with a great deal of gusto.

A play by 22-year-old Sam Shepard, the generally acknowledged "genius" of the OOB circuit, captures the central image underlying a good many of the plays in his one-acter, *Chicago.* A young man stands in a beat-up bathtub in the center of a bare stage, clad only in blue jeans. He reflects about life in a forlorn but funny mono-logue while his friends bustle past, elegantly dressed for business and vacation trips. His luscious girl friend in a sexy red wrapper gets into the tub with him briefly and nuzzles him cheerfully, then goes off just as cheerfully to take a job in Chicago. However, at the play's end, the characters all line up at the front of the stage in their smart uptown clothes in a zombie-like stance, confronting emptiness. It's evident that they're all, as it were, in the same tub. He cops out of the social scene, naked and infantile, and they bus-tle around within it. They don't try to make him join them, and he doesn't try to influence them. They all know everyone is faced with a void and trying to stave off terror, each in his own way.

Sex, in an impressive variety of forms, is popular on the OOB circuit. Homosexuality, incest, and sado-masochism are treated frequently and sometimes humorously. Unlike Broadway, which for the most part celebrates heterosexual domestic bliss or picks away long evenings at the problems of those lacking it, OOB plays it cool. The playwrights have the same sardonic acceptance of deviation as of psychic despair. In fact, sexual dislocation is usually a metaphor for philosophical distress. A good many of the plays take place in bed. The practical reason for this is that beds fill up a small stage interestingly and are easily obtainable without cost. But it's not just the practicality or the sexiness alone that makes for the popularity of the bed on the OOB circuit. In this theater, the bed is a metaphor for a lot of things. It is the place where people are supposed to come together, yet it's often where they find out how far apart they really are. It's the place of generation and regeneration, but when it doesn't serve those purposes, it becomes a symbol of sterility. It's a place of retreat, yet it is where we face nightmares.

Alienation, sterility, futility, nightmare—these are some of the psychic symptoms described in OOB plays. For example, in Robert Heide's play, aptly titled *The Bed,* two homosexuals are unable to rise from the bed although "sex is dead" for them. Also dead, according to the script, are time, God, and Nietzsche. Finally, one of the young men manages to get up and turn on the phonograph. He turns on a blasting rock-'n'-roll tune called "Anyway You Like It, That's Okay With Me, Baby." The two men sit motionless on the bed staring into space while the music, an all-pervasive yowl of pain vainly trying to conquer silence and void, assaults the audience's ears.

The playwrights, although they all consider themselves completely different from one another, are united in basic assumptions. Like the characters in their plays, they are "cop-outs" from their assigned seats on the gravy train of an affluent society. Educated and gifted, most of them are equipped to make a good living at a variety of well-paying writing jobs. They insist, however, that they "just can't" write Broadway material, advertising copy, or TV soap opera. They live in East Village pads, take odd jobs or small allowances from home, and get along more meagerly than is considered suitable for the well-brought-up middle-class young men and women they so evidently are. "It would be great to make Broadway money," says handsome 26-year-old Lanford Wilson wistfully. "You could do a lot with money, like buy a sauna bath or a million cases of gin, or all the paintings you want, but somehow. . . ." Wilson, who happens to be the most "traditional" writer on the OOB circuit, and is probably also the most polished and popular writer, recently had

a book of his plays published (*Balm in Gilead and Other Plays,*
Hill & Wang) and has had vague feelers from Broadway. However,
Wilson is having a ball in the coffeehouses, building his own sets
and directing his own plays, which he does superbly.

Among other regular playwrights for the OOB theater are Claris
Nelson, a pretty ingenue-type actress from California; Paul Foster,
a dark, intense Princeton graduate who works as a waiter in the La
Mama E.T.C., where his plays are produced, and Richard Falcone,
a drop-out from a highly-paid ad agency job. David Stern, a 16-
year-old Chicago schoolboy with braces on his teeth and a yarmulke
on the back of his head, will be introduced at the Cino this winter.

An important part of the OOB circuit is the Open Theater workshop, a group of actors, choreographers, painters and playwrights
headed by Joseph Chaikin and Peter Feldman. The group, which
occasionally puts on productions in La Mama E.T.C. and other
places, came together to study methods of improving the presentation of abstract or "nonobjective" plays. Like other OOB actors,
the members of this group have had conventional acting training,
but want to learn a style more suitable than the current "kitchen
realism" for what they consider to be the theater of the future.
"Method" acting just won't work for these plays, maintains Chaikin, who is himself a graduate of the Method school. "The actor in
the new type of theater must use his body more, and his voice in a
different way," Chaikin says. "The Method actor gets tied up in the
character's psychological knots, but in the new theater he keeps up
his awareness that he's an actor on a stage. Instead of portraying an
individual, he's a universal man."

This group pays out of its own pocket for the Spring Street loft
which is its headquarters, and the actors work in the OOB plays
for no money. Although everyone on the OOB circuit hopes that
some foundation money will soon spill over on them, they don't
seriously go after it. Their outcast spirit makes them ambivalent
about seeking help from the Establishment. "But one of these days
the foundations will wake up and realize that this theater is worthy
of encouragement," says Bill Regelson, an artist who designed and
directed the first full-length OOB spectacular, the avant-garde classic "King Ubu." "However, subsidies aren't the answer to the problem of creating live art. Lincoln Center is a good example. When
they wanted a talented director outside of the commercial mold,
they had to go to an impoverished group in a loft in San Francisco.

Now he [Herbert Blau] is saddled with a lot of expensive gimmicky equipment, a slick-chick audience and Establishment-oriented critics. He's got a big heap of concrete and glass that nothing can grow in. Culture centers are sterile and ugly. For growth to take place, there must be a warmth that seems to be generated best in a small private place, away from money and publicity. On the other hand, some money is vital to keep the thing going."

Joe Cino, who officially started the OOB theater seven years ago when he came down from Buffalo and opened his cafe on a side street in the Village, would agree about the money. His idea was to have a gathering place for friends, an art gallery, and a setting for poetry and play readings. He thought the profits from the sale of pastries and coffee would keep the tiny place going, but instead he found himself taking a full-time job to support the cafe. The play readings grew into a full-scale dramatization of Voltaire's "Candide." The actors, 16 in all, chased one another around the tables, for the stage was everywhere in the house. Gradually Cino, who had no special background in theater, started to get original plays from young writers and decided to try out a few. It worked well, and playwrights then started "crawling out from behind boards and under rocks." Now, like all other OOB entrepreneurs, Cino must read several scripts a week and has developed an astute eye for the good ones. When his place burned down last year, actors, playwrights, and audiences gave several benefits to re-establish him.

Because she knew some playwrights who had plays they couldn't get produced, Ellen Stewart, an attractive young woman who designs bathing suits (they bear the label "Elly"), decided to start a similar experiment in the East Village five years ago. She got caught in the wave of police harassment of coffee shops, which made no distinction between honky-tonk and intellectual establishments. She moved twice until she settled in her present location. Her solution to the harassment problem was to establish her place as a club. Members can have all the coffee they want and see as many performances as they want each week. Adored on the OOB circuit for phenomenal courage, energy, and faith in her playwrights, she led a group of actors, directors and playwrights to Europe last fall to set up a play series at the American Center for Students and Arts in Paris and in the Montmartre Jazz Gallery in Copenhagen. Miss Stewart believes Americans don't see their artists until Europeans recognize them, and she hopes the European response to the plays will be strong enough to make Americans aware of what OOB is doing. She is confident that the next genius of American drama will be born and nurtured on the OOB circuit.

The Hardware Poets, which started three years ago in its hard-ware-store loft, was given sanctuary last year by the Good Shepherd-Faith Presbyterian Church, which charges the group no rent. Additional expenses are met by a $4,000-a-year subsidy from its four founders—Elaine and Jerry Bloedow, Peter Levin, and Audrey Davis, all interested in acting, writing and directing.

Four years ago the Judson Memorial Church at Washington Square South set aside a $600-a-year subsidy for an arts program that would include dance and theater. The Rev. Alvin Carmines, assistant pastor at the church, directs about half of the plays and the other half are done by Lawrence Kornfeld. The kind of play done at the church was at first upsetting to some members of the congregation and earned it the label of "the beatnik church." "There was a bit of controversy for a time, but it was finally decided that if there was to be such a thing as an arts program it must be free and uncensored and that's the way it's been," says Mr. Carmines.

There was a similar situation at St. Mark's-in-the-Bouwerie, where Theater Genesis was established with a small subsidy, a little more than a year ago. Ralph Cook, director of the arts program at the church, now has complete freedom to select the plays he wants to do and to direct them or turn them over to another director. "The congregation came to see that the church is part of the community and the artist is part of the community," says Cook. "It is not Christianity or any religion to exclude the artist and what he has to say."

The OOB circuit is certainly here to stay for a while. Whether it will ultimately affect the course of American theater remains to be seen. However, it has already achieved success in its own terms by providing exposure for young playwrights and by initiating audiences into a new theater experience. Author-philosopher Paul Goodman, who has himself had several plays done on the OOB circuit, says: "Radically new theater, like any new art, cannot expect a mass-popular response, for it presents what is unfamiliar and is even actively resisted as meaningless, perverse, or dangerous. The sign of successful new theater is that the audience is torn between fascination and the impulse to walk out in disgust."

That's OOB, all right.

"Happenings" in the New York Scene

by Allan Kaprow

. . . If you haven't been to the Happenings, let me give you a kaleidoscope sampling of some of their great moments.

Everybody is crowded into a downtown loft, milling about, like at an opening. It's hot. There are lots of big cartons sitting all over the place. One by one they start to move, sliding and careening drunkenly in every direction, lunging into people and one another, accompanied by loud breathing sounds over four loudspeakers. Now it's winter and cold and it's dark, and all around little blue lights go on and off at their own speed, while three large, brown gunny-sack constructions drag an enormous pile of ice and stones over bumps, losing most of it, and blankets keep falling over everything from the ceiling. A hundred iron barrels and gallon wine jugs hanging on ropes swing back and forth, crashing like church bells, spewing glass all over. Suddenly, mushy shapes pop up from the floor and painters slash at curtains dripping with action. A wall of trees tied with colored rags advances on the crowd, scattering everybody, forcing them to leave. There are muslin telephone booths for all with a record player or microphone that tunes you in to everybody else. Coughing, you breathe in noxious fumes, or the smell of hospitals and lemon juice. A nude girl runs after the racing pool of a searchlight, throwing spinach greens into it. Slides and movies, projected over walls and people, depict hamburgers: big ones, huge ones, red ones, skinny ones, flat ones, etc. You come in as a spectator and maybe you discover you're caught in it after all, as you push things around like so much furniture. Words rumble past, whispering, dee-daaa, baroom, love me, love me; shadows joggle on screens, power saws and lawnmowers screech just like the I.R.T. at Union Square. Tin cans rattle and you stand up to see or change your seat

" 'Happenings' in the New York Scene" by Allan Kaprow. From *Art News*, Vol. 60, No. 3 (May 1961). © 1961 by *Art News* and reprinted with their permission.

or answer questions shouted at you by shoeshine boys and old ladies.
Long silences, when nothing happens, and you're sore because you
paid $1.50 contribution, when bang! there you are facing yourself
in a mirror jammed at you. Listen. A cough from the alley. You
giggle because you're afraid, suffer claustrophobia, talk to some one
nonchalantly, but all the time you're *there*, getting into the act . . .
Electric fans start, gently wafting breezes of "New-Car" smell past
your nose as leaves bury piles of a whining, burping, foul, pinky
mess.

So much for the flavor. Now I would like to describe the nature
of Happenings in a different manner, more analytically—their purpose and place in art.

Although widespread opinion has been expressed about these
events, usually by those who have never seen them, they are actually
little known beyond a small group of interested persons. This small
following is aware of several different kinds of Happening. There
are the sophisticated, witty works put on by the theater people; the
very sparsely abstract, almost Zen-like rituals given by another group
(mostly writers and musicians); and there are those in which I am
most involved, crude, lyrical, and very spontaneous. The last grew
out of the advanced American painting of the last decade and I and
the others were all painters (or still are). However, there is some
beneficial exchange between these three areas.

In addition, outside New York, there is the Gutai group in Osaka,
reported activity in San Francisco, Chicago, Cologne, Paris, and Mi-
lan, as well as a history that goes back through Surrealism, Dada,
Mime, the circus, carnivals, the traveling saltimbanques, all the way
to medieval mystery plays and processions. Of most of this we know
very little; only the spirit has been sensed. Of what *I* know, I find
that I have decided philosophical reservations about much of it.
Therefore, the points I shall make are not intended to represent the
views of all of those who create works that might be generically related, nor even of all of those whose work I admire, but are the issues
which I feel to be the most adventuresome, fruitfully open to appli-
cations, and the most challenging of anything that is in the air at
present.

Happenings are events which, put simply, happen. Though the
best of them have a decided impact—that is, one feels, "here is something important"—they appear to go nowhere and do not make any
particular literary point. In contrast to the arts of the past, they have
no structured beginning, middle, or end. Their form is open-ended
and fluid; nothing obvious is sought and therefore nothing is won,

except the certainty of a number of occurrences to which one is more than normally attentive. They exist for a single performance, or only a few more, and are gone forever, while new ones take their place.

These events are essentially theater pieces, however unconventional. That they are still largely rejected by most devotees of the theater may be due to their uncommon power and primitive energy, and to the fact that the best of them have come directly out of the rites of American Action Painting. But by widening the concept "theater" to include them (like widening the concept "painting" to include collage) it is possible to see them against this basic background, and to understand them better.

To my way of thinking, Happenings possess some crucial qualities which distinguish them from the usual theatrical works, even the experimental ones of today. First, there is the *context,* the place of conception and enactment. The most intense and essential happenings have been spawned in old lofts, basements, vacant stores, in natural surroundings and in the street, where very small audiences, or groups of visitors, are commingled in some way with the event, flowing in and among its parts. There is thus no separation of audience and play (as there is even in round or pit theaters), the elevated picture-window view of most playhouses is gone, as are the expectations of curtain-openings and *tableaux-vivants* and curtain-closing. . . . The sheer rawness of the out-of-doors or the closeness of dingy city quarters, in which the radical Happenings flourish, are more appropriate, I believe, in temperament and un-artiness, to the materials and directness of these works. The place where anything grows up (a certain kind of art in this case), that is its "habitat," gives to it not only a space, a set of relationships to various things around it, a range of values, but an over-all atmosphere, as well, which penetrates it and whoever experiences it. This has always been true, but it is especially important now, when our advanced art approaches a fragile but marvelous life, one that maintains itself by a mere thread, melting into an elusive, changeable configuration, the surroundings, the artist, his work, and everyone who comes to it.

If I may digress a moment to bring into focus this point, it may reveal why the "better" galleries and homes (whose décor is still a by-now-antiseptic Neo-Classicism of the '20s) desiccate and prettify modern paintings and sculpture which had looked so natural in their studio birthplace. It may also explain why artists' studios do not look like galleries and why, when an artist's studio does, everyone is suspicious. I think that, today, this organic connection between art and its environment is so meaningful and necessary that removing one from the other results in abortion. Yet, this life-line is denied continuously by its most original seers, the artists who have made us aware of it; for the flattery of being "on show" blinds them to every insensitivity heaped upon their suddenly weakened offerings. There seems no end to the white walls, the tasteful aluminum frames, the lovely lighting, fawn-grey rugs, cocktails, polite conversation. The attitudes, I mean the world view, conveyed by such a fluorescent reception is in itself not "bad." It is unaware. And being unaware, it can hardly be responsive to the art it promotes and professes to admire.

Happenings invite one to cast aside for a moment these proper manners and partake wholly in the real nature of the art and (one hopes) life. Thus a Happening is rough and sudden and it often feels "dirty." Dirt, we might begin to realize, is also organic and fertile, and everything, including the visitors, can grow a little in such circumstances.

To return to the contrast between Happenings and plays, the second important difference is that a Happening has no plot, no obvious "philosophy," and is materialized in an improvisatory fashion, like jazz, and like much contemporary painting, where one does not know exactly what is going to happen next. The action leads itself any way it wishes, and the artist controls it only to the degree that it keeps on "shaking" right. A modern play rarely has such an impromptu basis, for plays are still *first written*. A Happening is *generated in action* by a headful of ideas or a flimsily-jotted-down score of "root" directions.

A play assumes words to be the almost absolute medium. A Happening will frequently have words, but they may or may not make literal sense. If they do, their sense is not part of the fabric of "sense" which other nonverbal elements (noise, visual stuff, actions, etc.) convey. Hence, they have a brief, emergent and sometimes detached quality. If they do not make "sense," then they are heard as the *sound* of words instead of the meaning conveyed by them. Words, however, need not be used at all: a Happening might consist of a swarm of locusts being dropped in and around the performance space. This element of chance with respect to the medium itself is not to be expected from the ordinary theater.

Indeed, the involvement in chance, which is the third and most problematical quality found in Happenings, will rarely occur in the conventional theater. When it does, it usually is a marginal benefit of *interpretation*. In the present work, chance (in conjunction with improvisation) is a deliberately employed mode of operating that penetrates the whole composition and its character. It is the vehicle of the spontaneous. And it is the clue to understanding how control (setting up of chance techniques) can effectively produce the opposite quality of the unplanned and apparently uncontrolled. I think it can be demonstrated that much contemporary art, which counts upon inspiration to yield that admittedly desirable verve or sense of the un-self-conscious, is by now getting results which appear planned and academic. A loaded brush and a mighty swing always seem to hit the ball to the same spot.

The word "chance," then, rather than "spontaneity," is a key term, for it implies risk and fear (thus re-establishing that fine *nervousness* so pleasant when something is about to occur). It also better names a *method* which becomes manifestly unmethodical if one considers the pudding more a proof than the recipe.

Traditional art has always tried to *make it good every time,* believing that this was a *truer* truth than life. When an artist directly utilizes chance he hazards failure, the "failure" of being less Artistic and more Lifelike. "Art" produced by him might surprisingly turn out to be an affair that has all the inevitability of a well-ordered, middle-class Thanksgiving dinner (I have seen a few remarkable Happenings which were "bores" in this sense). But it could be like slipping on a banana peel, or Going to Heaven.

Simply by establishing a flexible framework of the barest kind of limits, such as the selection of only five elements out of an infinity of possibilities, almost anything can happen. And something always does, *even things that are unpleasant.* Visitors to a Happening are now and then not sure what has taken place, when it has begun or when it has ended, or even when things have gone "wrong." For by going "wrong," something far more "right," more revelatory, has many times emerged. It is this sort of sudden near-miracle which presently seems to be made more likely by chance procedures.

If one grasps the import of that word "chance" and *accepts* it (no easy achievement in our culture), then its methods need not invariably cause one's work to reduce to either chaos or a statistical indifference lacking in concreteness and intensity, as in a table of random numbers. On the contrary, the identities of those artists who employ such techniques are very clear. It is odd that by giving up certain hitherto privileged aspects of the Self, so that one cannot always "correct" something according to one's taste, the work and the artist frequently come out on top. And when they come out on the bottom, it is a very concrete bottom!

The final point I should like to make about Happenings as against plays was mentioned earlier, and is, of course, implicit in all the discussion—that is, their impermanence. By composing in such a way that the unforeseen has a premium placed upon it, no Happening can be reproduced. The few performances given of each work are considerably different from each other; and the work is over before habits begin to set in. In keeping with this, the physical materials used to create the environments of Happenings are of the most perishable kind: newspapers, junk, rags, old wooden crates knocked together, cardboard cartons cut up, real trees, food, borrowed machines, etc. They cannot last for long in whatever arrangement they are put. A Happening is thus at its freshest, while it lasts, for better or worse.

Here we need not go into the considerable history behind such values as are embodied in Happenings. It is sufficient to say that the passing, the changing, the natural, even the willingness to fail, are not unfamiliar. They reveal a spirit that is at once passive in its acceptance of what may be, and heroic in its disregard of security. One is also left exposed to the quite marvelous experience of being *surprised*. This is, in essence, a continuation of the tradition of Realism.

*   *   *

. . . The significance of the foregoing is not to be found simply in the fact that there is a fresh creative wind blowing. Happenings are not just another new style. Instead, like American art of the late 1940s, they are a moral act, a human stand of great urgency, whose professional status qua art is less a criterion than their certainty as an ultimate existential commitment.

It has always seemed to me that American creative energy only becomes charged by such a sense of crisis. The real weakness of much vanguard art since 1951 is its complacent assumption that Art exists and can be recognized and practiced. I am not so sure whether what we do now is art or something not quite art. If I call it art it is because I wish to avoid the endless arguments some other name would bring forth. Paradoxically, if it turns out to be art after all, it will be so in spite of (or *because* of) this larger question.

But this explosive atmosphere has been absent from our arts for ten years and one by one our major figures have dropped by the wayside, laden with glory. If tense excitement has returned with the Happenings, one can only suspect that the pattern will be repeated. These are our greenest days. Some of us will become famous and we will have proven once again that the only success occurred when there was a lack of it.

Such worries have been voiced before in more discouraging times, but today is hardly such a time when so many are rich and desire a befitting culture. I may, therefore, seem to be throwing water on a kindly spark in a chilly country when I touch on this note, for we customarily prefer to celebrate victories without ever questioning whether they are victories indeed. But I think it is necessary to question the whole state of American Success, because to do so is not only to touch on what is characteristically American and what is crucial about Happenings; it is partly to explain America's special strength. And this strength has nothing to do with Success.

Particularly in New York where it is most evident, we have not yet looked clearly at recognition and what it may imply—a condition that, until recently, has been quite natural to a European who has earned it. We are unable to accept rewards for being an artist, because it has been sensed deeply that to be such a man means that we must live and work in isolation and pride. Now that a new *haut mode* is demanding of us art and more art, we find ourselves running away or running to it, shocked and guilty, either way. I must be emphatic: the glaring truth, to anyone who cares to examine it calmly, is that nearly every artist, working in any medium from words to paint, who has made his mark as an innovator, as a radical in the best sense of that word, has, once he has been recognized and paid handsomely, capitulated to the interests of good taste, or has been wounded by them. There is no overt pressure anywhere. The patrons of art are the nicest people in the world. They neither wish to corrupt nor actually do so. The *whole* situation is corrosive, for neither patron nor artist comprehends his role; each is always a little edgy, however abundantly the smiles are exchanged. Out of this hidden discomfort there comes a still-born art, tight or merely repetitive at best, and at worst, chic. The old daring and the charged atmosphere of precarious discovery, which marked every hour of that modern artist's life, even when he was not working at his art, vanishes. Strangely, no one seems to know this, except, perhaps, the "unsuccessful" artists waiting for their day. . . .

To us, who are already answering the increasing telephone calls from entrepreneurs, this is more than disturbing. We are, at this writing, still free to do what we wish, and are watching ourselves as we become caught up in an irreversible process. Our Happenings, like all the other art produced in the last decade and a half by those who, for a few brief moments, were also free, are in no small part the expression of this liberty. In our beginning, some of us, reading the signs all too clearly, are facing our end.

If this is close to the truth, it is surely melodrama as well, and I intend the tone of my words to suggest that quality. Anyone moved by the spirit of tough-guyism would answer that all of this is a pseudo-problem, and is of the artists' own making. They have the alternative of rejecting fame if they do not want its responsibilities. They have made their sauce; now they must stew in it. It is not the patrons' and the publicists' moral obligation to protect the artists' freedom.

But such an objection, while sounding healthy and realistic, is in fact European and old-fashioned; it sees the creator as an indomitable hero who exists on a plane above any living context. It fails to appreciate the special character of our mores in America and this matrix, I would maintain, is the only reality within which any question about the arts may be asked.

The tough answer fails to appreciate our taste for fads and "movements," each one increasingly equivalent to the last in value and complexion, making for that vast ennui, that anxiety lying so close to the surface of our comfortable existence. It does not account for our need for "loving" everybody (our democracy) which must give every dog his bone; which compels everyone known by no one to be addressed by his nickname. This relentless craving loves everything destructively, for it actually hates Love. What can anyone's interest in *this* kind of art or *that* marvelous painter possibly mean then? Is it a meaning lost to the artist?

Where else can we see the unbelievable and frequent phenomenon of successful radicals becoming "fast friends" with successful academicians, united only by a common success and deliberately insensitive to the fundamental issues their different values imply? I wonder where else but here can be found that shutting of the eyes to the question of *purpose?* Perhaps in the United States such a question could not ever before exist, so pervasive has been the amoral mush.

This everyday world affects the way art is created as much as it conditions its response—a response the critic articulates for the patron, who in turn acts upon it. Melodrama, I think, is central to all of this.

Apart from those men in our recent history who have achieved something in primarily the spirit of European art, much of the positive character of America can be understood by that word. The saga of the Pioneer is true melodrama, the Cowboy and the Indian; the Rent Collector, Stella Dallas, Charlie Chaplin, the Organization Man, Mike Todd, are melodrama. And so now is the American Artist a melodramatic figure. Probably without trying, we have been able to see profoundly what we are all about through these archetypal personages. This is the quality of our temperament which a classically-trained mind would invariably mistake for sentimentality.

But I do not want to suggest that the avant-garde artist produces even remotely sentimental works; I am referring more to the hard and silly melodrama of his life and his almost farcical social position, known as well as the story of George Washington and the Cherry Tree, and which infuses what he does with a powerful yet fragile fever. Partly it is the idea that he will be famous only after he dies, a myth we have taken to heart far more than have the Europeans, and far more than we care to admit. Half-consciously, though, there is the more indigenous dream that everything is in the *adventure;* the tangible goal is not important. The Pacific coast is farther away than we thought, Ponce de Leon's Fountain of Youth lies beyond the next everglade, and the next, and the next . . . meanwhile let's battle the alligators.

What is not melodramatic, in the sense I am using it, but is disappointing and tragic, is that today the vanguard artist is given his prizes very quickly, instead of being left to his adventure. And he is, furthermore, led to believe, by no one in particular, that this was the thing he wanted all the while. But in some obscure recess of his mind, he assumes he must now die, at least spiritually, to keep the myth intact. Hence, the creative aspect of his art ceases. To all intents and purposes, *he is dead and he is famous.*

In this context of achievement-and-death, an artist who makes a Happening is living out the purest melodrama. His activity embodies the myth of Non-Success, for Happenings cannot be sold and taken home; they can only be supported. And by their intimate and fleeting nature, only a few people can experience them. They remain isolated and proud. The creator of such events is an adventurer too, because much of what he does is unforeseen. He stacks the deck that way.

By some reasonable but unplanned process, Happenings, we may suspect, have emerged as an art that can precisely *function,* as long as the mechanics of our present rush for cultural maturity continue.

This will no doubt change eventually and thus will change the issues of this article.

But for now there is this to consider, the point I raised earlier: Some of us will probably become famous. It will be an ironic fame fashioned largely by those who have never seen our work. The attention and pressure of such a position will probably destroy the majority of us, as it has nearly all the others. Our kind of artist knows no better how to handle the metaphysics and practice of worldly power than anyone else. He knows even less, since he has not been in the slightest involved with it. That I feel it necessary, in the interests of truth, to write this article which may hasten the conclusion, is even more fatefully ironic. But this is the chance one takes; it is part of the picture. . . .

Yet, I cannot help wondering if there isn't a positive side, too, a side also subject to the throw of the dice. To the extent that a Happening is not a commodity but a brief event, from the standpoint of any publicity it may receive, it may become *a state of mind.* Who will have been there at that event? It may become like the sea-monsters of the past or the flying saucers of yesterday. I shouldn't really mind, for as the new myth grows on its own, without reference to anything in particular, the artist may achieve a beautiful privacy, famed for something purely imaginary, while free to explore something nobody will notice.

The Juggernaut of Production

by Gordon Rogoff

In the autumn of 1958, Lee Strasberg told the members of The Actors' Studio that he was feeling worried and belligerent about the emphasis on individual excellence that seemed to have become the entire *raison d'etre* of the Studio, an emphasis which he considered to be taken at the expense of the concept of the ensemble. "We lose the sense," he said, "of serving the theater." His worry, seen then or now, could be easily understood by the most casual observer of the American theatrical scene. His belligerence, then and now, can not be so easily understood, since it is not readily apparent to the naked—or should I say hungry?—eye.

Belligerence implies the will to change, and in the case of those who would lead American theater, the will to do more than change a way of work. The word belongs to the vocabulary of war. A real war now would raise greater issues than the question of individual excellence. It would be devoted to overturning all that is dead, deader, deadest in what passes for a system in American theater. It would not be so much a revolution as a civil war, a war between those old contenders, Mammon and Art. Strasberg, moved as he was by a vague discontent with a "system" in which his Studio continued to be only a workshop and never a theater, and by his strong feelings for such institutions as the Moscow Art Theatre and the Group Theatre, felt in turn, a belligerence vague at best and meaningless at worst. He was correct in his observation that the sense of serving the theater had been lost in the pursuit of individual excellence. Characteristically, he did not permit his concern and his warlike nature to carry him to the next logical question: serving *what* theater? And so this season [1963], we have, with the creation of The Actors Studio Theatre, only the latest in a line of group the-

"The Juggernaut of Production" by Gordon Rogoff. From *Tulane Drama Review*, Vol. 8, No. 1 (T21, Fall 1963), 130-156. © 1963 by Tulane Drama Review, and reprinted with their permission and the author's.

aters to whom that question must, in all harshness, be directed. What theater are you? Do you serve the idea of a Broadway theater or—and here I borrow freely from Francis Fergusson—the Idea of a Theater?

A review of plays and productions in New York is not ordinarily the most appropriate forum for a discussion of trends. The strictures of space are reason enough to avoid generalities: the critic is usually sufficiently wise to leave grand design to others, or to save it for a time when he is not called upon to assess plays as isolated phenomena. I am not so wise. I prefer, at least at the beginning of my term of trial, to suggest a general framework for discussions of particular performances. The language for this framework is drawn, for the sake of sense and convenience, from politics, since I am unable to witness events apart from their wider sources. There is no attempt here to claim startling originality, nor am I so foolish as to propose a rigid system of analogy: Robert Whitehead and Elia Kazan are simply in charge of the new Lincoln Center Repertory Theatre; they are not—in spite of their press releases—alter egos for John F. Kennedy and Lyndon Johnson. What I propose for myself and for those readers whose enmity is not immediately aroused, is a simple structure of analogy that admits only that American theater does not happen outside of American society. This means that, as the society shows both variety and conformity, so will its institutions; that, as the society shows less of one and too much of the other, so again will its reflectors, the institutions; and finally, that, as the society today is characterized by its politics of the possible, its end of ideology, so are its institutions characterized by their lack of daring, their compromises with the heart of creative matter, their absence of ideas.

We are a severely damaged people. Under the shadow of a flag, we can be led to do or not do almost anything, no matter how outrageous. In the politics of the possible, nuclear war gradually becomes more probable if the neutron bomb is developed, since only people will be killed and property can be spared. We lay waste our powers not by arguing to make killing impossible, but by arguing about how we can make it more efficient—and therefore always possible. Just so do we estrange ourselves from those impulses that drive us to recognize our uniqueness, making us reach not for what is possible but for what would seem to be impossible. The process of estrangement has the appearance of a philosophical encirclement to the estranged man: he wishes to be himself, but he cannot accept himself with all his complexity unless he withdraws at least partly from himself, accepting the will of the group; but in the group he soon obliterates himself. The image is terrifying. Estrangement catches estrangement by the tail.

A man knows that he can be himself only by being himself, a unit alone, not lonely, just apart. Yet he can only *be,* that is, exist, as a unit in an organized society. Should he attempt the impossible —existence outside of what is externally organized—he may for a blinding moment feel that he *is* himself *by* himself *for* himself, but he is in immediate danger of ceasing to be. He needs the group more than the group needs him. In the Middle Ages, when a man belonged to at least two groups—his family and his guild—yet made his living *from* himself (that is, whatever he produced from his own labor), the definitions of self were more clearly marked. Even the word *individual* had a different association: Raymond Williams, in *The Long Revolution,* tells us that it meant *inseparable,* implying a direct and continuous relation with others. The word underwent a semantic change, a change meant to reflect the spirit of a time when a man was likely to make his living less from himself and more by means of working machines created and owned by other men. The machine has a life of its own; the organized industry has a life of its own; within the capitalistic structure, the industry is the pillar of society; and yet *individual* no longer means *inseparable.*

This paradox, or—if you will—dialectical tension, is the source of the modern individual's existential anguish. As he becomes more and more aware of his separability from the group, he becomes more and more dependent on the sovereignty of the group for his life. The separable unit is separable only insofar as he is inseparable. He is expected to have an identity, and indeed, he severely needs an identity; but the group is not concerned with the inherent truth of his identity, only with the statement of *an* identity, however foreign it may be to the basic nature of the man himself. Thus, the paradox is compounded: the fundamental group—our nation-state—involves us in its actions in the name of freedom and individualism; yet the more we get involved in and moved by its actions, the more we lose our sense of personal control. The "philosophy" by which we live is individualism; the consequence of this "philosophy," however, is a new feeling—the feeling that we are not living, that we have lost our individuality. Only by playing the politics of the possible, we say, can we put ourselves outside danger, for in this manner we accept the group at it exists, we do not try to impose on the group what *ought to be,* we exist with what is. But in so doing, we as unique beings cease to exist.

Scarred, then, by a philosophy that is not a philosophy, by a way of life that alienates us from our own way of living, by a fragmentation of self that makes us easy cannon fodder for the manufactured needs of the group, we then move into our smaller groups, our arenas of work. It is not surprising that in these groups we live a life cycle—or living-death cycle—in microcosm: we enter in order to flower as individuals; we work within the group in order to help the group work as an individual, as one man; we settle, therefore, only for what is possible; if not, we are expected to leave the group; faced with two choices each leading toward extinction, we may try to destroy the group; we are now failing ourselves as creative individuals and we are failing the group; we choose *not* to destroy the group, but to leave it; we retain, at great cost, some measure of individuality; the group continues to *be* for a time, but without the individuality that derives from individuals; it does only what is possible; it soon becomes impossible to *be* anything more than a *name*.

I have described, as you can see, a condition that is more relevant to our lives than any plays, productions, or theaters can pretend to be. But it *is* relevant to the condition of dramatic art in our country. Indeed, the cycle I have described represents in general outline the history of *group* theaters in the United States. (Not arbitrarily, I am excluding from discussion those theaters that have developed a reputation in the fifties because, with the arguable exceptions of The Living Theatre in New York and The Actor's Workshop in San Francisco, they have made no attempt to behave as group theaters, that is, as permanent ensembles. They are, more accurately, one- or two-man operations devoted to fund-raising, bricks and mortar, and local reputation. They have produced plays, but they have not yet produced an idea of a theater.) The chilling truth that emerges from our group-theater history is that we do not build ensembles, we build houses with only the outline of personal character; houses laced with good intentions, but unsupported by any substructure of good ideas. We begin forming our groups with a vague yearning toward European models, but like the heroines of Henry James, while we may love and envy Europe, we are in time suffocated by its masks and manners, which for us can have no native meaning. We are, after all, fugitives from Europe, not exiles. Our rooted wish is to forge a new world. The pull away from the old world acts like our pull away from the group: the wish may be rooted in change and isolation, but the need is linked with the past and others. We try, unsystematically, to define our groups by fighting the psychological definition of our national character. For Francis Fergusson, the Idea of a Theater meant the dramatic art of Shakespeare and Sophocles, developed "in theaters which focused, at the center of the life of the community, the complementary insights of the whole culture." What I am suggesting, then, is that in the United States, a group theater, even if centered in a community, can only suggest the complementary insights of the whole culture by not behaving as a group at all.

This is a severe view, difficult to accept by anyone who cares, as I do, for what is present and potent in the real world of dramatic poetry. Yet, even as it must be accepted, it can be challenged. What is pernicious in the politics of the possible is that it neither accepts nor—by its very nature—can it challenge this view. It speaks for change, yet it works for the status quo. By playing it, whether in national or theater politics, we succeed only in rendering impotent our drive for what is new, changing, and individual. We are not free men philosophically until we reach for ideas and ideals that make demands upon the status quo. Art, above all, as Robert Brustein reminded us in his assault on The Actors' Studio, "is the politics of the impossible." [1]

We are faced, then, with problems of so complex a nature that it is not surprising we should so often refuse to admit them. They are expressions of opposites that must be forced to live with one another: we know from European history that group theaters can serve the drama as no individual productions can, so we wish to make group theaters; opposed to this is our own special character, inherently hostile to the sovereignty of the group; we are trying, therefore, to do the impossible; yet opposed to this we persist in doing it by playing the politics of the possible. What reconciliation can be made must be attempted on the basis of reversing energies in order to bring some order *into* the chaos. Yes, we should say, art *is* the politics of the impossible, but we are simply attempting the wrong impossible for us, that is, groups modeled on European theaters. The right impossible would recognize the anarchy in our nature, and make group theaters on a new, almost literally anti-group basis.

Let me be clear about what I am not saying. I am not saying that there is nothing to be learned from Europe or the past. Far from it: for only one example, we should never forget that great theaters— from the House of Molière to the House of Brecht—have been built around great dramatists. To know Europe, however, is simply

---

[1] *The New Republic* (December 1, 1962).

not to know—or *acknowledge*—ourselves. Yearnings are no substitute for personal confrontations. And so I *am* saying that we should know and confront our own character, our own individuality. And I am not saying that I know precisely how this can be done.

What I do know is how it can *not* be done. It can not be done by building on Broadway or by following the model of Broadway production. If we choose to make our impact by boring from within, we shall only succeed in boring. I have taken the time to indicate a framework for a continuing discussion in these pages because the random appraisal of productions in New York has little value any more unless it is related to goals that reach far beyond what seems possible on Broadway. There are artists working professionally and irregularly in New York today, yet they rarely succeed in producing works of art. What I propose to do now and in subsequent issues [of *Tulane Drama Review*] is to scrutinize their work closely in order to separate the parts of production: writing from directing, directing from acting, designing from writing, and so on. In this way, I hope further to illuminate the areas lying between art and commerce, intention and mendacity, achievement and self-deception. In New York, we are each of us daily witness to a war that rages so intensely on a smoky battlefield that, like Tolstoy's reeling warriors, we are not often capable of seeing what weapons are being used, who is getting murdered, or why we are fighting in the first place. The production of plays has taken the form of a huge juggernaut, inexorably bearing down upon all the embattled, confused, and angry fighters. The casualties are overwhelming. The waste is unforgivable. In bringing to bear some measure of critical reason on the plays that are produced, we are saying, in effect, that good work doesn't follow directly from the fact that we are working, that meaningless activity bears no relation to intelligent action, that movement on a treadmill is really paralysis, and that, therefore, the juggernaut must be halted, peace must be declared.

*   *   *

Many people suffer in the destructive wake of the juggernaut, but no one more than the playwright. He is the classic culprit, his "crimes" viewed either with cool condescension or cold fury. If the first, he is seen only as a stubborn, unrealistic, perhaps too literary man; if the latter, he is a conspirator in disguise, a wicked man bent upon upsetting the morals of the audience or the proven talents of the actors, directors, and designers. The tradition of baiting the playwright has a long and dishonorable history; in the case of

Shakespeare, a tradition barely overthrown. (He is still not safe: the late critic of *The New Yorker,* Wolcott Gibbs, notably lacking in ideas or a subject he could call his own, passed himself off as a sophisticated wit by hating all the plays of Shakespeare; and only this year, a critic for one of the more reputable, unyellow British newspapers, complained of the "boringness" of *The Tempest,* a play he considers beyond salvation by even the most talented theater people.) We should, of course, take the condition of Shakespeare as a useful hint. If today we are able to view a poor production of *King Lear* without declaring the play to be unactable—a hoary belief we know to be unsound—it is because we are willing to accept the possibility that we are not necessarily seeing Shakespeare's play, only a *version* of his play. We are, not surprisingly, more generous now toward Shakespeare than to our contemporaries. The reputation of *Hamlet* as a play survives the most outlandish whims of directors, but *Andorra*—just to take one vulnerable example from this season's carnage—will not be so lucky. We are rarely free enough to imagine new plays in other productions. We damn the playwright before we distribute the blame.

This is not to say that the playwright is untouchable, only a victim and never a clod. It is just that the juggernaut hits the *good* playwright first. For Walter Kerr, in 1956, when *Waiting for Godot* was produced, "there was something profound on the stage of the Golden Theatre . . . and that something was Bert Lahr." Beckett will survive the blush that Mr. Kerr ought to be wearing by now, but not all playwrights—particularly the young, local writers—are likely to be so hardy.

The juggernaut has a way of astonishing and then exiling those who are serious. Its main tool is compromise, and since, by its inexorable nature, it can not be stopped, somebody's vision has to be sacrificed. The onslaught may begin with what seems to be only a tiny compromise, an infinitesimal speck of matter in a universe of suns, moons, and milky ways. On the subtlest (and lowest) level, it may be the power of the playwright's agent, still believing Broadway production a signal honor, to persuade the writer that his play *deserves* Broadway. From that decision, there is likely to follow a long line of choices, of so simple or oblique a nature that they are only too easy to accept.

We are all familiar with the form: a star is hired, the star wants to be loved, or, at the least, look pretty or handsome; the director, a star in his own domain, noted earlier for his nimble choreography, or his evocative stage designs, or his days as a subleading man,

then casts the other roles from a vast pool of auditioning actors
who, while they are unsuitable for various mystic reasons such as
height, weight, noses, and hair, nevertheless demonstrate to the director which scenes "work" and which will need surgery; then the
designer sees the play in various shades of blue framing an enormous network of tin cans stapled together to form a harrowing symbol of the webs of yesteryear, leaving room for the actors to move
only from downstage right to downstage left; the producer wants
more laughs, egged on by the press agent who needs a gimmick;
Variety's out-of-town reviewer thinks it is bad B.O. for Broadway,
and calls for more carefree musicals; the star stops talking to the
director; the director won't talk to the playwright; the playwright
is going stir-crazy in his hotel room, having forgotten what his play
is about after a dream in which he saw someone else writing his
play; the blue-haired ladies who sell theater parties think the play
needs more heart; the costume designer is going through her Wat-
teau period; the *New York Times* seems to be on a "kick" for philosophical musicals concerning Chinese integration; and the *Herald
Tribune,* using its inside knowledge on how *not* to write a play,
says that atmosphere will never replace good, solid craftsmanship,
and furthermore, there may be a touch of anti-clericalism lurking
in the third act; the play closes after five performances, leaving the
star to Hollywood, but not before granting interviews that express
great relief to be free of that "turkey"; the director has already
been called to Philadelphia to salvage a musical; the playwright
goes back to basket weaving; and the producer, gazing myopically
over the great literary reaches of Europe, Asia, the Middle East,
Africa, Latin America, and continental United States, declares sol-
emnly that there are no new plays anymore, and since even poor
musicals can make money, he plans to produce still another, a nasty
little number starring Merman and Martin, based on the Bobbsey
Twins. We heave a sigh and drop a tear, grateful that at least one
man remains a success unto himself.

My distortions are only slightly out of focus, for the juggernaut
makes all things, in the theater of the possible, quite possible indeed. There is a story making the rounds in New York this season
that one playwright, awaking on the morning after the homicide,
realized with a shudder that it was a matter of great urgency for
him to bring himself face-to-face with his typewriter to begin the
physical work of writing a new play. In pain, but saved by a still,
small voice within that spoke for work instead of extinction, he sat
before the machine, placed the paper, and wrote, without conscious

meditation, instinctive words born from revulsion: "The curtain rises—on a bare stage."

But if the playwright learns only through the most bitter experience, the actors, designers, and directors—who *need* production work more than the playwright—scarcely ever learn. If it is true, as Steven Marcus said of Sinclair Lewis, that in America "nothing fails like success," it is perhaps even sadder and truer that our artists rarely find any success in failure. This year we have seen mayhem on the battlefield that left behind the wounded works of such playwrights as Max Frisch, Jack Richardson, Tennessee Williams, William Inge, and Lillian Hellman. None of them—with the possible exception of Frisch, who could not have known the full force of the juggernaut in advance—is without a share of responsibility in the disaster, and Miss Hellman is one of the few writers for our theater who cannot complain of directors and producers who are stronger men. But regardless of where we assign the greatest responsibility, we can not fail to ask at least two questions: if the plays of these writers remain so unimproved, so unrealized, or so awful after the time, attention, and money devoted to Broadway production, then isn't there something absurdly perverse in that *mode* of production? And if this is so, why do these same producers, directors, actors, designers, *and* playwrights propose to return to Broadway some day soon in the same mode to commit similar murder?

Frisch, of course, may never come back. The loss, being ours, need not trouble him for long. He has seen *Andorra* in a production by Fritz Kortner at the Schiller Theatre in West Berlin that is said to be the living image of the play he imagined and wrote. What he saw here in a production by Michael Langham was surely beyond his imagination, and if we are to believe Kenneth Tynan, who found the play a "near-masterpiece" in Berlin,[2] it could not have been recognizable. Langham's greatest effort seemed devoted to the game of parading so many productional conceits and imitations before our eyes that we would be tricked into imagining that we were actually seeing a production with an idea. Boris Aronson designed a solid, specific, white papier-maché mountain town, whose very real walls were being whitewashed as the curtain arose by a girl wielding a dry brush and an empty can. The set had bulk without reason, rising planes without purpose, and a general sense of obstruction that seemed to force all the action into only three small downstage areas. The cast presented a world ruled by Babel, ac-

[2] *The Observer* (January 6, 1963).

cents clashing like so many uncoordinated cymbals in a high school band. And of Horst Bucholz's callow pose or Hugh Griffith's rolling eyes, there is nothing to say, except to beg Henry Irving to return from his grave and show them how it was done. That this was not *The Bells*, I can not be certain. George Tabori's "adaptation" (why are novels translated and plays adapted?), sounding like *Fledermaus* in English, domesticated what we have reason to believe was a drama developed with more subtlety and a grander line. Tynan speaks of a scene in which the father staggers home from the tavern, ironically hooting the word "Jud." What we saw was a family scene around a kitchen table in which, at one barely emphasized point, the father rants *angrily* that wherever he goes he hears the word "Jew." It is a measure of our ruin that everything we touch turns to family.

*   *   *

Jack Richardson's first Broadway production, *Lorenzo*, was no less calamitous. One might as well cast Joan Sutherland as Boris Godunov as choose Alfred Drake for the role of a remnant Pierrot-Charlot. Lorenzo is first cousin, once removed, of the wandering clown played by Nils Poppe in Ingmar Bergman's *The Seventh Seal*. For quicksilver we had lead. For wit we had archness. For wonder, worry. For resignation, exhaustion. For feeling, voice, voice, and more voice. But it takes more than one miscast actor to massacre a play, though that will do ample service for a start. Fritz Weaver brought a clean attack and a swiftly responsive imagination to his role of the general, but where was he to go with his second act aria, confined as he was to the top turret of David Hay's sickly-green jungle gym, an obstacle course of would-be bed springs designed to make immovable actors even less mobile? Weaver chose abdication, joining at last the atmosphere of lassitude that pervaded Arthur Penn's weirdly indecisive production. Richardson's play, let me not mistake it, is far from masterful. His welcome gift for rhetoric too often overcomes his even stronger gift for the comically grotesque, sound swimming away from sense. We should not, however, be either so greedy or so ungrateful as to expect great plays from men so young; the poet in love with the words he wrote for *Love's Labour's Lost* had a long life in the theater ahead of him, even though the Taubmans of his day would have declared him too green for the theater. What we have a right to expect is that our theater will bring some initial concept to the production of new plays, transliterating into the terms of the stage those views and feelings in Richardson (and Frisch) that are bold, imaginative, and freshly written.

*   *   *

Bertolt Brecht, too, is a new playwright on Broadway, though, unlike his colleagues this season, he appears to be a critical, if not a very popular, success. His new play, *Mother Courage and her Children*, comes to us only twenty-four years after it was written, which as time travels on Broadway, is probably a quarter of a century sooner than customary practice. In this respect, the production would seem to stand outside the main path of the juggernaut. To do it well, even to do it at all, is to challenge the terms of our production values at their very center.

First, there is the didactic purpose of the play, about which Brecht took pains, as was his custom, to be clear. It is not, as we would ordinarily have it, a simple statement, easily agreeable to all of us, blandly against an abstraction called war. A production should show, said Brecht, "That big business (Geschäfte) is not conducted by little people. . . . That war, which is an extension of business by other means, makes human virtues fatal, even for those who possess them. . . . That for the waging of war, no sacrifice is too great." [3] Brecht's ironic adaptation of Clausewitz's theory that war is an extension of politics by other means is just one hint among many that he was concerned with the perversions and vocabulary of capitalism. If, like Pavlov's dog, we froth at the mouth when we hear that word, we shall then either try to erase its presence from the world of the play, or pretend in our fashion that Brecht was an artist who "transcended" the "limitations" of his views. As dogs, however, we miss the human force of his ideas.

Brecht was a Marxist. But to acknowledge this is not to say that he was ever *able* to be a Communist in what we might call the Pavlovian manner. During the middle period in which he wrote such "didactic pieces" as *The Exception and the Rule* and *The Measures Taken,* he was surely attempting a repression of his own instincts in favor of service to a more orthodox Left view; yet even in these plays there is occasional ideological ambiguity. It isn't necessary or sound to press amateur psychology into the study of Brecht. We have only to look at the line of his development in the plays

[3] *Courage-Modellbuch* (1949).

themselves. What emerges—despite his adaptation to necessity by making his theater in East Berlin—is a strong absorption in two aspects of Marxism that tend to get lost in the distorting mirror of the cold war: the dialectical thinking process (to which I shall return later); and the classical humanism, which is a tradition far different from the Soviet managerial, conservative adaptation with its surrender of the individual to a collective fixation.

Marx saw man in terms of his potential, not as an alienated thing; a man for whom the process of production exists, not a man who exists for the process of production. When Marx described his concept of real independence and real freedom, he might well have been describing the condition of Mother Courage in Brecht's play: "Private property has made us so stupid and partial that an object is only *ours* when we have it, when it exists for us as capital or when it is directly eaten, drunk, worn, inhabited, etc., in short, *utilized* in some way; . . . . Thus *all* the physical and intellectual senses have been replaced by the simple alienation of *all* these senses; the sense of *having*." [4] That Anna Fierling at least has the courage to *be* in spite of all the evidence against the value of being, is, perhaps, the one point that continually appears to throw the play back into the romantic, heroic theatrical tradition against which Brecht was reacting. But this is clearly in line with the tension in the play that keeps it in motion—a living, vibrant demonstration of an individual *not quite* becoming someone better during the course of history. The theatrical presentation of this Marxist view of our existence and our potential follows logically from Marx's philosophy (though we would never know it if we assign responsibility to Marx for the unresonant obtuseness of "socialist realism"). Brecht clears the stage for action, an action that springs from our primal reasons for making plays: to show man to man. His play is a demonstration of how one person under capitalism does not learn from experience, and it is performed—or ought to be—for the purpose of entertaining us by teaching us to learn. Where Brecht failed was not in his art, which is alive, complex, comic, and deeply felt; but in any illusion he had that this play could be performed by a company of players before an audience which, like itself and Mother Courage, is conditioned by alienation from real responses *not* to learn. In short, as Brecht knew well, our theater and our audience ask invariably that a character learn some-

---

[4] Karl Marx, *Economic and Philosophical Manuscripts*, 1844, trans. T. B. Bottomore; incorporated in Erich Fromm's *Marx's Concept of Man* (Frederick Ungar, 1961), p. 132.

thing in a play, and they ask this because they do not wish to learn anything themselves.

This philosophical challenge to our values is only the first problem for the American director of Brecht's play. The aesthetic challenge is, of course, closely related. If we are unwilling to accept a major character who does not learn, we are equally unwilling to accept the manner in which the author shows us her *lack* of development. It is at this point where a critic such as Tynan, meaning well for Brecht and feeling something close to pity for the director and actors, tends to review the audience and daily reviewers rather than the production. It is a forgivable evasion, but no less an evasion for all that. Audience, reviewers, and players mirror one another, not as immutable beings beyond hope, but as people conditioned by the same atmosphere, the same sources of dullness. They are no different from soprano fanciers and note counters in the opera house, delighting in all that is on the surface, all that is visible to their very naked eyes, all that can be heard by untrained ears. The only crime is a note sung sharply. If it is sung loud when the composer specifies soft, if it is held long when the composer asks for the music to move on, they either do not know or do not care to know. What is fast, loud, raucous, pushy, and superficially alive is quite enough for them. What may take its time, glowing from within, at the service of the composer, is not merely unwanted, it is a genuine affront. They use the theater as a drug, to make them high, to give them excitement. Slow movements are interludes, fast movements are fun. Pace—interminable, unmeaning pace—is our theatrical god: if the two hours' traffic upon the stage does not move fast, it moves us not at all. We come to the theater, whether behind or before the footlights, in order to get out of it as soon as possible. What we don't see, we don't want to see. What we see, we want to see quickly. As Tynan observed of a young Chelsea girl who was "bored to death" by *Mother Courage* in the performance of the Berlin Ensemble, she should have said "bored to life."

Brecht, aware of the danger, reacting himself against the undivine afflatus of so much German art, warned the actors of the Ensemble in March 1956 to play with lightness and clarity in their London performances:

> The acting must move along quickly, lightly, and vigorously. We should act, not in order to excite, but in order to prevent lagging, not only to play at a fast tempo, but to think quickly. We must watch the tempo of the dialogue, but we must add to the dialogue our own lightness of touch. Replies should not be given in a dilatory

way, as if we were offering somebody our last pair of shoes, but we
must act as if we were throwing the ball quickly back and forth.[5]

This message has the characteristic Brechtian double edge, which
was undoubtedly easy for the Berlin actors to comprehend quickly:
it calls for speed, but it is opposed to excitement; thus it assumes
the ability to give quick thinking a steady, sensible, interior rhythm.
This, like the art of true *bel canto*, is the art of propelling the
melodic line forward while holding it back.

Now, this may make sense to Maria Callas, but not necessarily to
most of her contemporaries, so far removed are they from the techniques and feelings of *bel canto*. Equally, it made sense to Brecht's
actors, trained by him in terms of a purpose and an aesthetics upon
which all, in different measure, could agree. But, as we have seen,
we think and we move differently. The usual terms we read in connection with Brecht do not reach our sensibility as they must have
reached his colleagues: "epic theater," "alienation effect," do not
illuminate our vision of Brechtian production; indeed, they seem to
obscure it.

Again, Brecht wished to be understood, even in the West. It is
not accidental or insignificant that, just before his death, he was
trying to replace the term "epic" with "dialectical" in order to describe his theater. As Peter Demetz observes in his introduction to
a group of critical essays, "Brecht complained that people without
a sense of humor would never be able to understand Hegel's dialectics. One might also say that these people will never be able to
grasp some of the most vital implications of Brecht's art." [6] In other
words, his art is comedy that bases its drama on interior argument,
the clash of opposites, the tension that exists between two seemingly
irreconcilable ideas. These dialectics are at once the source of the
humor, the drama, and therefore, the very *form* of the writing. We
are compelled, if we are willing, to listen to every line in order to
"hear" its opposite:

Cook. . . . He's completely unsound.
Mother Courage. And you're completely sound?
Cook. And I am completely sound. Your health!
Mother Courage. Sound! Only one person around here was ever sound,
      and I never had to slave as I did then. He sold the blankets off the

children's beds in autumn. You aren't recommending yourself to me if you claim to be sound.

Suddenly—and *we* really must be quick to catch it—the virtue of "being sound" is called into question; indeed it is so completely overturned that we can no longer so easily assume it is a virtue.

In this manner, Brecht sets little dialectical time-bombs underneath all our dearly held notions, theoretical and theatrical. To our actors, he seems to be saying: Withdraw yourself, do not be emotional. Yet is he really saying this, or more accurately, is he saying this alone? Is it not, in fact, a matter of *not* denying emotions, but admitting into your sphere different kinds of emotions, related perhaps, not just to the individual, but to the individual as he is connected to other people and the world around him?

> In all the feelings and actions of your characters
> Look for the new and for the old! [7]

Which is to say there *are* feelings. Brecht, as Martin Esslin reminds us, was revolted by "the cramped and convulsive style of acting which is still widely prevalent in the German theater, where actors still tend to be rated according to the violence, the frenetic intensity of the emotions they portray. The frantic *Ausbruch* (outburst) represents the highest peak of acting by the adherents of this style. The Brechtian actor is always loose-limbed and relaxed, always clearly in control of himself and his emotions." [8] Brecht was quite simply traveling down the main stream of modern art, which has by now extended Pope's "The proper study of Mankind is Man" to mean more fully that "The proper study of Mankind is Man's relationships." Once again, Brecht tried to make himself clear: "The conventional theater . . . drives its action from the nature of the characters," [9] he said, whereas for him "the smallest social unit is not the single person but two people." [10] Or as Esslin explains: "The study of human *nature* is thus replaced by that of human relations." [11]

To our directors and designers, he was equally dialectical. He seems to be saying: Withdraw yourself from magic and illusion.

[7] Brecht, *Poems on the Theatre*, trans. John Berger and Anna Bostock (Scorpion Press, 1961), p. 10.

[8] Martin Esslin, *Brecht* (Doubleday, 1961), p. 131.

[9] *Ibid.*, p. 133.

[10] Brecht, *A Short Organum for the Theatre*, trans. Eric Bentley, in *Playwrights on Playwriting* (Hill & Wang, 1960), p. 94.

[11] Esslin, *Brecht*, p. 133.

But again, does this mean only what it seems to say? Does it deny the existence of illusion or the fact of magic? In the Courage-Model-book, he recognizes the illusionary implication of even a bare stage:

> The completely empty stage with its circular horizon . . . un-doubtedly creates the illusion that the flat landscape represents heaven. *On the other hand,* it doesn't necessarily follow that because *a poetic emotional response is required* from the audience, it is fully accomplished by this *kind of illusion.* The *illusion can be created* quite easily by the mere acting of the actor. [My italics.]

Which is to say that there *is* illusion in the theater, and that Brecht simply wished to make it in a different way, a way purer to him, though not necessarily usable in all kinds of plays. It is, in a very precise sense, a new way of speaking to an audience: deriving the-atrical "magic" not from the denial of your materials, but by admit-ting them, and absorbing them into the details of your performance. To the director, his instruction is plain enough:

> . . . the spectator
> Should see
> How cunningly you prepare for him
> Should see
> The tin moon come swaying down
> And the cottage roof brought in.
> . . . .
> Let him discover
> You are not conjuring
> But working.[12]

To the designer, he advises specific means:

> Give us light on our stage.
> How can we disclose
> We playwrights and actors
> Images to the world in semi-darkness?
>   . . . The little bit
> Of night that's wanted now and then
> Our lamps and moons can indicate.
> And we with our acting too can keep
> The times of day apart.
> . . . .
> Therefore flood full on

[12] Brecht, *Poems on the Theatre,* p. 12.

> What we have made with work
> That the watcher may see. . . .[13]

I have stressed dialectics because, without them as a tool of thought and work, one gets—at best—only bare Brecht without a passion. Implicit, then, in this attenuated appraisal of Brechtian purpose and practice is my view that Broadway has not only failed Brecht, but that it would have been astonishing if it had done otherwise. It is possible in this context to haggle, like Mother Courage, over details; to bargain over the chances available for making a better deal out of the production under the Broadway circumstances —a different star, perhaps, some stronger men, a more sensual feeling for props, light, and music. But haggling, as Courage might have learned, only plays the game according to the rules of the system, changes nothing, and sometimes leaves even greater disaster in its wake. Broadway, it is clear enough, is professionally able to cope with the details of craft, but is professionally bankrupt of ideas, and therefore, incapable *organically* of coping with Brecht.

Mother Courage on Broadway, lacking Brecht's double edge, settles for Jerome Robbins's half-world, neither all Broadway nor all Berlin, not *alienated* so much as *semidetached*, a world in which Brecht's apparently simple means are mistaken for simplicity. It is really a sad world, wilting when it should be moving, punching hard when it should be nudging, winking when it should be insinuating. A beautiful, sweeping cyclorama is flooded with light only at rare moments. Indeed, the tricks of production are always more apparent than the work: the sources of light and music remain hidden; light is adjusted for atmosphere; and the scene changes are masked partially by the flashing of huge slides on the cyclorama showing modern scenes of war and deprivation. Yet ironically, where mechanical "magic" would seem to be mandatory—that is, through the use of a turntable—we have none. And so the play moves sideways and backwards, in and out of the wings, but never *around* the mechanistic chronicle of the war. Bancroft's props are new, yet she plucks a *real* capon. Young actors grey their hair and stuff themselves with pillows, but just as they are trapped in a static world that advances yet never progresses, so do they never grow old or fat. It is all as if Robbins, following the choice of Prospero, abjured his own rough magic, but did it long before he had absorbed Brecht's so potent art.

With the casting of Anne Bancroft, we have a variation on the

[13] *Ibid.,* p. 14.

half-world: the good actress in the wrong part. In theory, there is
no one more admirable in our cautious theater than the actor who
moves away from the pattern expected by his audience, stretching
his range by exploring new characters. But between the theory and
the practice lies the playwright. And for him, the actor's stretch
can mean his play's distortion. Several years ago, in a public performance at The Actors' Studio, Miss Bancroft showed that she
could sling Eliza Doolittle over her formidable young back, and
belt out "Just You Wait" as if she had been Mermanizing all her
life. Belting, however, is not for Brecht. Nor is toughness without
irony. Miss Bancroft's "Curse the War!" returns us flatly to the
German—and American—theater of outburst which Brecht so carefully abhorred. She is a woman of great, good, open feeling, only
inches away from inviting us into her wagon for a glass of beer.
Since she can't do that, she does the next worst thing: sentimentally
and tragically, in the great tradition of every theater but Brecht's,
she learns from the experience of her losses, though, of course, like
her wagon on the unmoving stage, she has no place to go.

It is not that there is only one way of playing Courage. The Mod-
elbook makes it clear that, between Therese Giehse and Helene
Wiegel, Brecht was pleased with both, suggesting an idea from one,
a moment from the other. Esslin quotes an observer at the Ensemble
who noticed that at rehearsals "everyone is allowed to state his
opinion. The actors make all sorts of suggestions to the producer." [14]
In our theater, based as it still is on individual expression, everyone
states his opinion on the telephone or in a bar. Thus, we do not see
an ensemble on Broadway or a sense of collaboration. We see
Jerome Robbins in a collaboration with himself where he has re-
nounced much of himself while still clinging to a New York director's natural inclination to *save* the playwright. Unfortunately, it
was not possible for the playwright to save him. Brecht, in fact,
might have supplied the last warning to Robbins and the last critical word for us:

> To observe
> You must learn to compare.
> To be able to compare
> You must have observed already.
> From observation comes knowledge.
> But knowledge is needed to observe.
> He who does not know

[14] Esslin, *Brecht*, p. 138.

What to make of his observation
Will observe badly.[15]

*   *   *

He who observes well and knows what to make of his observation
would not, in 1963, produce Eugene O'Neill's *Strange Interlude*.
Yet that is precisely what The Actors' Studio has done, presumably
with Strasberg's consent, in its first organized public effort to realize
the "theater intention" of which he spoke in 1958, "transmitting,"
as he said, "a technical concern, a knowledge of craft . . . all for
a sense of theater which transmits a new image of what theater can
do." On the surface, first, what are the salient elements forming this
new image? They are a very old and tired play by O'Neill that
might have been at home in the serialized pages of the *Woman's
Home Companion*; our decade's "O'Neill director," José Quintero,
who has never been an active participant at The Actors' Studio;
and eight stars, only two of whom (Geraldine Page and Geoffrey
Horne) have been *regular* workers at the Studio during the past
five years. The new image, then, would seem to bear the marks of
a somewhat older image, one with which we are all rather familiar,
the image of Broadway; in fact, of our old friendy enemy, the juggernaut. When is change ever not the same?

The image of O'Neill haunts what lies beneath the surface. "The
more he attempts," said Eric Bentley, "the less he achieves." And
of course, the disease is catching. Bentley sounded the warning and
named the perpetrators of the bloody deed, but, as always, his words
went either unread or unheeded. What he said then is central to the
choice made by The Actors' Studio, and so I quote from it at length:

> What is surprising is not that his [O'Neill's] achievements fall be-
> low Dostoyevsky's but that critics—including some recent rehabilita-
> tors—have taken the will for the deed and find O'Neill's nobler
> "conception" of theater enough. "Conception" is patently a euphe-
> mism for "intention" and they are applauding O'Neill for strength-
> ening the pavement of hell. . . . No brows are higher indeed than
> those of the subintelligentsia. They spend their time seeking sublim-
> ities, works that provide the answers to the crying questions of our
> time, impassioned appeals for justice, daring indictments of tyranny,
> everything sure-fire. Seek and you shall find: a writer like O'Neill does
> not give them the optimism of an "American Century," but he pro-
> vides profundities galore, and technical innovations, and (as he him-
> self says) Mystery. Now, there is a large contingent of the subintelli-

---

[15] Brecht, *Poems on the Theatre*, p. 19.

gentsia in the theater world. They are seen daily at the Algonquin and nightly at Sardi's. They don't all like O'Neill, yet his "profound" art is inconceivable without them. O'Neill doesn't like *them*, but he needs them, and could never have dedicated himself to "big work" had their voices not been in his ears telling him he was big. The man who could not be bribed by the Broadway tycoons was seduced by the Broadway intelligentsia. . . . A hundred novelists have dealt more subtly with hidden motives than O'Neill did in his famous essay in psychological subtlety, *Strange Interlude,* a play that is equally inferior as a study of upper-class Americans.[16]

Seduced by bigness, by Conception, we build the longest bridges, the tallest buildings, the greatest supermarkets, and the most pretentious theaters. It can scarcely surprise us, then, that our latest group theater begins by producing not just O'Neill, but the worst O'Neill, thus revealing its scattered brains, born and nurtured at the University of Sardi's. Yet even so, why the worst O'Neill? After all, while forcing the American theater to take itself seriously, he did write several plays whose scope was narrow, but whose feelings were true. The answer is that The Actors' Studio Theatre is not only in competition with Broadway, it is also fighting a miniature civil war with its "renegade" director, Kazan, and his yet unborn Lincoln Center Repertory Theatre. And Mrs. O'Neill, quixotically as usual, has granted performing rights to Lincoln Center for most of her late husband's plays. Hence, the choice on the part of the Studio was probably as unstoppable as the high, aesthetic adaptation of the juggernaut that they are promoting: nobody asked, Why O'Neill?, and everybody agreed to the one Big Play available. Quintero, no doubt, came wrapped in the package.

The most notorious conceit of actors and directors is that they can make out of what they merely call "old-fashioned" something "interesting" and "exciting." It is true that in theatrical history there have been actors who have often made successful vehicles out of material that was muddy-mettled, obvious, unsubtle, and poorly wrought. Duse, Bernhardt, Irving, and Salvini spent half their acting lives rising above their plays, though Duse, bless her, had the care and agony of feeling to regret the dumbness of many of her warhorses. "To save the theater," she said, "the theater must be destroyed, the actors and actresses must all die of the plague. They poison the air, they make art impossible. It is not drama that they play, but pieces for the theater." [17]

[16] Eric Bentley, *In Search of Theater* (Knopf, 1953), pp. 230-231.
[17] Quoted in Toby Cole and Helen Krich Chinoy, *Actors on Acting* (Crown, 1949), p. 413.

All disasters, too, are "interesting" and "exciting": fires, murders, sinkings, the Final Solution of the Nazis. But the mind of an infant psychologist struggling with unmalleable vocabulary to say next to nothing in more hours than you can nod your head at is neither interesting nor exciting. What *is* morbidly interesting and quite unexciting is the response of the audience. It laughs at line after line in the play, particularly the earnest interior monologues of Marsden, the writer who doesn't face life. Good citizens all, they are not laughing at O'Neill's ineptitude, but at what they think *must* be his sense of humor. Perhaps they feel compelled to laugh *with* him because the structure of their willed belief in him as a playwright would otherwise collapse about their dulled wits.

How, after all, can this play be taken seriously? Some of its apologists give it H for Humanity. Have we removed ourselves so far from our own humanity that we can mistake these emotional zombies for real people? In the name of "realism" we are asked to believe that for twenty-five years the major figures in the play are concerned with only *one* subject: Nina, her men, and the ghost of Gordon Shaw. For plot, we have that one night in bed that is so important to Grandmother's melodrama. For background, we are supposed to be in the Northeastern states after World War I. But since the play spans the period between 1919 and 1944 and was written in 1926-27, we are emphatically out of time and out of place. The liberty is not pardonable, since O'Neill, characteristically unable to transform his material, never tries to make out of the timelessness and placelessness a clear, poetic abstraction. He is simply on stage relentlessly clinging to his commonplace story. Plot, unimportant in itself, assumes importance only when it is not ignored. Incredibly, however, O'Neill believed in his plot, and undeveloped it from act to act to act. His language, springing neither from a responsive ear nor from a remotely poetic imagination, remains stillborn. And yet he writes on and on. In theory, his interior monologues are means to reveal the *real* drives, feelings, and thoughts of the characters, designed to give dramatic pause simply because we are to wonder when these inner thoughts will be brought into open and direct confrontation. But the inner and the outer voices are monotones, the inner always asking only one question: shall I or shall I not tell him or her what I am thinking? But *we* know what O'Neill should have known, that *if* anybody were to do so, there would be mercifully five or six fewer acts to endure.

What we do endure are nine acts—count them—of blood lines, streaks of insanity, dangerous alliances, undigested biology, voodoo psychology, instant pregnancy, and a conveniently placed heart attack. It is a triumph of unreal realism, all plays in one, and no play in itself.

Quintero and the actors, carrying the conceit of group work as far as it can go, rehearsed all these no-plays in the regular four-week period called for by the union rules of Broadway. What is old-fashioned, they may have thought, would seem merely quaint, overshadowed by the peculiar and subtle insights they would bring to the story and characters. What is old-fashioned, perhaps; what is *not*-fashioned, never.

Following the logic of the occasion, they offer *not*-production. The play drifts aimlessly from interior monologue to exterior dia-logue, developing no rhythm among the characters, and only occa-sionally imposing a sense of moment, and then only through the use of spotlights and slow fades. The four leading actors—Page, Pat Hingle, William Prince, and Ben Gazzara—can be commended for endurance and bravery under long, long fire. Only Page, how-ever, shows signs of breaking loose from the pervasive monotony. When she is on stage, we may still be suffering through soap opera, but it is never soap of the broadcast variety. She is an actress who must be watched at all times. Indeed, she forces you to watch, on the occasional off-chance that she may tear herself away momen-tarily from O'Neill's imprisoning emotions. Early in the first scene, there is a startling instant when she appears to be edging toward a way of making the interior monologues a part of the action, some-thing propulsive; a sharp *frisson,* a shiver overcomes her body as she comes out of thought to hear her father who has been talking. But she seems almost afraid to develop Nina beyond the confine-ments of the play and production. She withdraws noticeably from playing the cool, calculating, compellingly beautiful and attractive creature called for by the fantasy of the text—the Nina that these three supposedly different men would find so intensely appealing. She works, as always, with great ease and a rich emotional response to the situations, despite their unyieldingness, but in the end, she leaves behind no sense of character.

Ironically, even with Page, and certainly with all the others, it is not the "truth" of inner life that one remembers. It is what they impose from the outside: Page's wigs, the way in which she so un-comfortably manipulates her cigarette holder, the manner in which her body undulates in the same rhythm from scene to scene, year to year; Franchot Tone's vocal quaver, oddly reminiscent of Lionel Barrymore's worst days; Betty Field's wig and obvious discomfort with the "dialect"; Hingle's bluff heartiness; Gazarra's wooden walk, his doctor's character observed not from life as we know it, but from medicine as we see it on television; Prince's royal posture; Jane Fonda's gritty voice and fluttering arms, reaching for feelings as artificial as her make-up; and finally, Geoffrey Horne's vain efforts to keep his veins from popping while he is squeezing for emotion.

The set offers a clue to the "mystery" of the play's clumsiness. David Hays, still obsessed with greens, has mounted "period" furniture on a huge turntable. For the scenes, however, he bisects the turntable with wallpaper backdrops, cutting the playing area, pressing the play down to size; which may, of course, be wise, in view of the nature of the material. Yet when the set, dimly lit, begins to turn, there is a sudden sense of air and space that is at once beautiful, fluid, and expressive. The play, earthbound, lacking rhythm and movement, suddenly and swiftly looks as if it is capable of taking wing, transforming itself, transcending the weight of its heavy-lidded prose. And then, just as suddenly, it is all over. Page, lying languidly on a chaise, spinning from upstage to downstage, will, we hope hopelessly for a moment, keep on turning, moving the play into some other arena, some kind of battleground where life is scrutinized, felt, and imagined, freely seen, freshly observed—in short, that the play will be swept mysteriously into a land that O'Neill scarcely knew, and then, not until the years of his pretense had passed.

*   *   *

Thus do we have a new group theater on Broadway.

To make plays successful on Broadway, one must join the juggernaut. There is no other way. On occasion, financial success may be matched by a production performed, directed, and designed with flair and confidence. But the ambition and scale of artistically successful work on Broadway must always be small. When large work, seriously intended, is swept into the path of the juggernaut, we invite serious trouble. Invariably, when we are staking our largest claims, we choose artistic traps as our business bedfellows, enlisting ourselves in the cause of several fallacies and confusions: we believe our own press releases, indeed, they are even more real to us than what we see every day; we believe that good intentions and fine achievements are the same; and finally, we believe that the play is *not* the thing. In short, we believe that our observation, in Brecht's terms, must be faulty before we feel ready to succeed! At odd moments, we may indeed be successful with *an* audience, and protected by our narcissism, even feel successful within ourselves. But, like Narcissus, all we have really done is gaze upon our features in the pond, only to fall in and drown from our unconsciousness.

After the congratulatory reviews of *Strange Interlude* were published, Strasberg remarked to the members of the Studio, no doubt in the spirit of jest, that "artistically we are a financial success." Every court, perhaps, must have its jester. But jesters were wise, and Strasberg is purported to be the King. Well, the King is dead and the jester is neither sagacious nor amusing. American theater has its unfair share of "realistic" men, confounding art with a witch's brew of money, and it needs no more. The last laugh, jester, is not really on us. It is on that foolish figure, the self-indulgent, group-joining, individual American artist who has lost his individuality while crowning his corruption with a dollar sign.

The Drama Is Coming Now

by Richard Gilman

The spirit of an age is known to reveal itself in everything that the age conspires to say about its engagements with itself. We have spoken about ourselves, which really means that we have spoken *to* ourselves, more characteristically, more obliquely, more problematically, in painting and sculpture than in the other arts. Here our dialogue has been driven by a greater underground fury, frustration in apparent freedom; here we find the aggressive jest and the sense of exhausted yet tenacious conventions still to be overcome. The novel and the film are only occasionally used for their proper purposes, and when they are they approach the graphic arts and become our autobiography. The rest is noise. It used to be that the other arts aspired towards the condition of music, but it is more nearly true to say that they now wish to reach the condition of painting and sculpture. Picasso, Jackson Pollock, and Brancusi— with their solid, unhistorical, and non-explanatory objects, their breaking of the mirror—are the sovereign exemplars.

And what about the theater? Even more heavily bound as it is to the social, to "communication," than the forms it resembles most, fiction and the cinema, it has fallen steadily behind an age in which the social is undecipherable and communication, like sleep, is impossible if you set out to achieve it. Where once the stage was the unparalleled means of a society's gaining a sense of itself and of all destiny, of life's winning through to formal and self-replenishing vision, it has become in all but a handful of its manifestations a wearisome repetition of what so many of its remaining devotees, like lovers blind to the withdrawal of love, continue to insist it is supposed to be. If it were not for the handful of plays (and they are the best plays of our time) that declare themselves to be other than

"The Drama Is Coming Now" by Richard Gilman. From *Tulane Drama Review*, Vol. 7, No. 4 (T20, Summer 1963), 27-42. © 1963 by Tulane Drama Review, and reprinted with their permission and the author's.

what drama has always been taken for, we would be too bored and dispirited even to go on thinking about it. Yet there is something to think about, indeed by now something to overtake.

What we have to catch up with, we who are concerned with the theater and particularly with the theater in the United States where it has perennially suffered from the conviction that beauty originates in the pocketbook of the beholder and is a matter of seduction, is, at the very least, a consciousness of what has been happening to the bases of drama. We need an articulated consciousness, one that spreads among the practitioners and invades the theaters or, at any rate, one that cannot help being heard no matter what its efficacy will be allowed to be.

No one thinks we can create a new drama by fiat or speculation or through aesthetic manifestos or manuals of more promising techniques. But it remains true that we may impede the arrival or growth of any possible theater of truth and substance simply by failing to rid ourselves of the accumulated and inherited notions, which come more and more to resemble prejudices, which we have relied on up to now to carry us past the difficulties in the way of understanding the nature of dramatic art. In *Six Characters in Search of an Author* there is this admonition: "The drama is coming now, sir, something new, complex, most interesting." As spectators, participants, and evaluators we have not even begun to deal with the changes that have already taken place, much less prepare ourselves for what is newer still.

In America, of course, apart from the hermetic activity of the professionally enslaved, we almost never deal with new aesthetic phenomenon until they have overwhelmed us with their multiplied presence, until, that is to say, they have become aesthetic norms. We continued to talk about Hemingway (and still do) chiefly in terms of his preoccupations, his values, obsessions, and possible neuroses until long after it was evident that his importance lay in his having changed the face of prose. *Axel's Castle* was a revelation to most of us, but the miracle was that nobody before Wilson had appropriated the material that had been lying so long at hand. Today we steadfastly ignore the new French novelists, who are doing the most interesting work of the moment, and make a mountain out of an artistic molehill of a novel like *Ship of Fools*.

We write about the movies as sociologists or technicians or chroniclers of nostalgia, and mourn or praise like warring philosophers the disappearance of the human image from modern painting. Except in regard to poetry, where we have been blessed (or cursed)

with the New Criticism's unflagging attentiveness, we have never
had anything like that close, public, reciprocal relationship between
aesthetic theory and practice such as the French, to take the supreme
example, have never failed to keep up. There are those of us who
are embarrassed or dismayed by such a liaison, but are we better
off for having adhered instead to the two-fisted, red-blooded propo-
sition that those who can, do and those who can't, teach?

The drama has suffered more than the other arts from the dis-
juncture between thought and activity that is so characteristic of
our cultural life. The American drama is itself almost mindless;
we weep for the intellectual deficiencies of Miller and Williams
and for the existence of O'Neill as our monument to the hair-
breadth victory of naked will and raw energy over language and
idea, a victory that nevertheless leaves the major laurels on other
brows. But our theater also suffers from a great reluctance to being
thought about, except in the most sanctified and unoriginal ways.
If the stage in America has produced so little that is permanent,
revelatory and beautiful, one reason for that is surely its aversion,
which resembles that of "masculine" Americans to poetry or practical businessmen to Harvard theoreticians, to being discussed as
an art, or at least as an art whose lineaments cannot be traced in
all the standard, echo-bequeathing textbooks. If we set out to discover the art of drama on the theater shelves we are led to taking
seriously Robert E. Sherwood and Sidney Kingsley, Lillian Hellman, William Inge, and Paddy Chayefsky.

It is doubtless also true that the notorious fate on American
stages of the most important and life-giving European drama—our
mangling, perverting, or simply letting go down the drain every
valuable accession from abroad, from Ibsen and Chekhov to Brecht,
Lorca, Beckett, Ghelderode, and Genet (we all have our memories
of anguish in this regard)—stems far more radically from a failure
of intellect, from a refusal to believe that intellect has anything to
do with theater, than from a deficiency of mechanical skills or
technique (which is in the end, however, almost nothing but a
question of a certain kind of intelligence).

Intelligence is the last virtue we seek in our directors of "significant" foreign plays, for example. "Theatrical sense," éclat, professional briskness, inventiveness of the order of those star salesmen
who "put over" a new product—these come first by a wide margin,
on Broadway and, with its atrocious timidity and pretentiousness,
off-Broadway as well; and it is a measure of our hopelessness in the
matter that when we do decide to make a gesture in the direction

of mind we apotheosize a director like Tyrone Guthrie or José Quintero or Elia Kazan, bowing to them as if they were the Platos of the theater, when the truth is that they have become, if they were ever not, its Walt Disneys and Cecil B. DeMilles.

We have absorbed the European novel into our own, we have taken over and now outdistanced European painting, but a chasm remains between our theater, our conception of drama and theirs. We still do not understand what they are about; and we go on believing that we can effect our regeneration without such under-standing. We wish to come to life again, or for the first time, with-out recognizing what the theater's true life is in our time. The point is that if the plays of Ibsen, Strindberg, Shaw, Chekhov, Pirandello, Brecht, Beckett, Ionesco, and Genet are permanent and inexhaustible, in themselves and especially in comparison with any-thing we have offered the world's stages, it is not simply because this European drama exhibits a greater complexity or a more direct involvement with crucial existence than our own, but because these plays in their various modes approach the theater as a means of *knowing* and not merely as a means of expression.

(But of course we may continue to comfort ourselves with the knowledge that the world makes a bigger thing of our accomplish-ments than some of us do. The world is wrong. If it pays extrava-gant homage to O'Neill, Williams, Miller, and now Albee, it is partly because an illusion is at work, the illusion of refreshment or inspiration from primitive sources common to minds tired of thought and subtlety, and also to minds that have never known them; the illusion that led Gide to call Dashiell Hammett our greatest novelist and other Frenchmen to adulate Horace McCoy; the illusion that leads a culture like Israel's, from the other ex-treme, to specialize in O'Neill in the belief that he is the shortest way back to the ancient Greeks and so to high "seriousness" on the stage.)

In Pirandello's *Six Characters* there is another moment of warn-ing and illumination. At one point the step-daughter protests against the attempt of the father, and by implication of the drama-tist who has placed all six "characters" in existence, to make their story theatrically viable. "He wants to get at his 'cerebral drama,'" she cries out, "to have his famous remorses and torments acted; but I want to act my part, *my part!*" The speech functions as one of the elements building the play to the realization of its theme, which may be described as the suffering produced by the conflict between levels of reality. But in its ironic suggestion that it is just the exigencies of the theatrical impulse that endanger the possibility of arriving at truth, the speech has a wider reference: it is expressive of the situation of modern drama, caught in a self-consciousness which it must draw upon to give itself strength, no longer straightforwardly celebrating the mysteries or dilemmas of existence but having moved to a position among them.

The speech also throws light on some of the problems of drama criticism in an age when the textbooks are exceptionally useless. We are still heavily involved, despite all the evidence to the contrary which continually arranges itself under our noses, in the fixed notion of drama as the enactment of passions, "cerebral" or otherwise, "famous" or, as is increasingly the case, quite the opposite. We go on thinking of a play as a structure in which to trap, shape, control, exemplify, and give significance to the major passions or to their perversions, which we further expect to embody themselves in the form of characters who will then work out their destinies along the unreeling line of a plot.

Yet if anything is true about drama as an art it is that it has passed through a transformation—has pressed its way through one —which has brought it to the condition of denying the usefulness of the passions as material, or at least their usefulness as long as they remain mummified within the inherited rigidities and spent predictabilities of traditional characterization and plotting. And this is one of the results of a more profound process. The drama, like the other arts, was alienated from itself and its immediate ancestry and then, subsequently, it recovered its own being through self-mockery, wit, fantasy, aggression, and ironic handling of its materials.

It should be a commonplace by now that all the representative art of our time is marked by a questioning—implicit or otherwise, comic mostly, extravagant, remorseless—of the very nature, purpose, and validity of art itself. We see this in the whole of twentieth century art, from Picasso, Stravinsky, and Joyce to Kafka, Pirandello, Brecht, Mann, the surrealists, Jackson Pollock, the pop painters and sculptors (who are representative of the latest twist of the knife upon which art is impaled when it repeats itself too long) the a-novelists, Beckett, Antonioni, Ionesco, Nabokov, and Genet. This questioning is what fixes "modern art" and most radically separates it from what came before. From Ibsen's *When We Dead Awaken* to the poems of Wallace Stevens to Mann's *Doctor Faustus* the testing and interrogation of art can be observed in many concrete instances. But even when it is not the direct subject of the work it informs the creative action throughout the modern period. And that this examination stemming from doubt and despair should have led to a revivification of the imagination and its forms is surely one of the paradoxical glories of our notably inglorious age.

Pirandello was one of the most conscious of the artists who have made the imagination do new duty, struggling at each moment with its treacherous inclinations and forcing it back to the business of truth. To act out a cerebral drama or to present us with remorses and torments, *passions* which are arbitrary and selective and therefore certain to do violence to the wholeness of truth, the stepdaughter in his play is saying, is to make it impossible for me to act *my part,* my truth, which I only wish to offer as the direct revelation of myself, the unmediated history of what has happened, and not the dramatization, reductive and distorting, of someone's idea of the way things happen.

The tension is between art and life, between knowledge and actuality, and the spiral of irony and paradox rises to an extreme height because of the fact that the girl is of course a dramatic creation to begin with. As such, she is fighting for her life within a play which is in turn fighting for its life within a larger play—the play *itself*—which is struggling for its own existence . . . that is to say, struggling towards a dramatic mode which will enable it to overcome the obstacles blocking the way to truth.

The step-daughter wishes, in other words, not to be a character, an arbitrary creation, but an identity, a reality, in the same way that drama, in Pirandello's practice, as in that of every other serious playwright of our time, wishes not to be the reflection of life, its staged version, but a reality, a counterpart or analogue. To act out known passions is to persist—as the most vigorous and original recent drama has told us by negation and new steps—in being the reflection of a life that in its loss of self-knowledge and confidence desires only to be handed back mirror images. These passions are useless because they are encrusted with a type of language that no longer describes the feelings themselves; beyond this they are fixed in those various flows of actions that have been repeated again and again because it is thought that there is no other way to present them. And it is these conventions, operating in the name of emotions, that serve to prevent any renewal or resummoning of passion from showing itself to us.

The analogy is, of course, with abstract painting's movement of repudiation and changed aims, its creation of a universe in which shapes, colors, and lines exist in their own right and not as the attributes or properties of objects that have their definition in the world of fact outside art. Such an analogy should not be carried too far; the best contemporary plays are not to be distinguished by their abstractness (the attempts at creating a theater of pure abstraction, in the manner of the experiments at the Bauhaus, the work of a playwright like Jean Tardieu, the Dadaists, or even Ionesco's slim, half-hearted, and mostly theoretical efforts in that direction, have resulted in not much more than some specimens of curiosa). Drama is nothing if not concrete. But there clearly are affinities between the relinquishment of subject in most recent painting and sculpture and the abandonment of character and the accompanying revolution in the concept of plot, character's milieu, that have come to be the characteristic features of certain dramas in our time. In both cases it is a matter of coming back to the truth, which lay disguised and impotent under the automatic functioning of convention. It is necessary to sketch the course of drama's entire revolution before returning to this rediscovery.

The theater is a way of knowing, a playwright is a mind. It has been more than fifteen years since Eric Bentley published *The Playwright as Thinker,* still one of the two or three most valuable works of American dramatic criticism, yet the only thing that seems to have happened is that we know the names now and have made uncertain visits to some of the places his pioneering on other shores opened up. The premise was so firm and lucid, the demonstrations for the most part so irrefutable. "The playwright must be a thinker not only if he wishes to be a propagandist. He must be a thinker if he wishes to be a great playwright." And once again, "every great writer is a thinker—not necessarily a great metaphysician but necessarily a great mind. Among the recognized great playwrights of the past there are no exceptions to this rule."

And yet we go our mindless way, chattering about "commitment" and "responsibility" as if they were not the most intellectually arduous endeavors, screeching about "robustness" and "passion," praising the most intellectually shoddy plays for their "power" or "vitality" or "sense of life," praising worse ones for their "thoughtfulness," unable to distinguish between thought and thoughts-in-drama, unable to take the yoke of "playwright of social ideas" from Ibsen, continuing to write such nonsense as Walter Kerr's dictum that the drama of ideas is one "in which people are digits, adding up to the correct ideological sum," and never seeing more than piece-meal and spasmodically that the drama in our time rides a revolution in ways of knowing and that its procedures follow stringently from that.

The Playwright as Thinker rose out of the observation that modern drama (1880 was Bentley's starting point, although he took the necessary look back to Kleist's and Büchner's practice and Hebbel's and Schiller's theory) has been much more concerned with ideas than the drama of any previous age. If in fact ideas are the essence of modern drama, this did not mean, Bentley was at pains to point out —"pains" is devastatingly mild; "torments" would be more accurate —that these plays have been aridly intellectual or that they are lacking in emotions or sensuousness. What it did mean was that at a certain point in the nineteenth century, with Wagner and especially Ibsen, drama identified itself with the rising critical spirit: that attitude of analysis and questioning the pursuit of which meant a reconstitution of forms. From then on ideas, or more broadly, thought, became increasingly important as the substance of the revived theater. This was dangerous thought which attacked and threw up alternatives to the settled habits of mind and sight of both the audience and the theater which had for so long served it as a rite of confirmation and solace.

In Robert Brustein's splendid chapters on Ibsen and Strindberg[1] from his . . . *The Theatre of Revolt* (a little that encompasses something even broader than Bentley undertook) we can see how this spirit of repudiation and urgent inquiry grew into the full-scale rebellion it has constituted ever since. The history of the theater over the last seventy-five or eighty years is in fact the history of that rebellion, but it is also the history of the refusal to recognize that the rebellion is all there is. For no art except the film possesses greater resources for the masochistic rejection of its own best possibilities than does the drama; that it is also theater makes it possible for it to resist revolution behind its physical arguments, its stages that must be enlivened and its rows of seats waiting to be filled, its economic exigencies and enforced obligation to what is immediately assimilable. The revolution remains outside, like the one in Genet's *The Balcony*; within, the life of illusion continues, the hall of mirrors goes on throwing back to its patrons the reflections they have always known.

Nevertheless, the revolution remains all there has been and all there is, even while the Pulitzer Prizes and Critics' Awards go on

---

[1] Robert Brustein, "Ibsen and Revolt," and "Male and Female in August Strindberg," originally in *Tulane Drama Review* (Fall 1962 and Winter 1963).

being punctually bestowed on what is mostly non-existent. Being a rebellion of a double kind, throwing off desiccated theatrical practices in the wish to cast off the dead image of itself that life had been putting on stage, it necessarily changed the forms of drama at the same time as it changed its subject. This is of course what happens in every transformation in the arts, yet the drama seems to have difficulty in understanding that new forms and new subjects arise together and that the avant-garde, far from imposing itself like an invention, appears, as Ionesco has written, "of necessity . . . it is self-generated when certain systems of expression are exhausted, corrupt, too remote from a forgotten model." No, it is not drama that fails to understand this but theater, that heavy institution to whom extreme conservatism is thought to be necessary for survival.

The well-made play depended for its acceptance on the belief that existence itself is well-made and that there is pleasure in witnessing clever demonstrations of the fact; the theater of intrigue, amorous confabulation, naked and solipsistic action, detection and denouement, and narrow psychological realism, depended on men's desires to see their lowly irrelevant dreams rehearsed on their physiognomies and psychic maps projected in a drama of repetition, reassurance, or that sort of titillating dangerousness that is also ultimately reassuring. When the drama of thought arose it was as a repudiation of such purposes and with the momentum of new ones. And just as it was the new purpose of Picasso and Stravinsky —their refutation of established belief and understanding, detectable behind the strange sounds and sights—that was so disturbing to their first audiences, so in drama it was the new intentions as much as the changed forms that "theater-lovers," professors, and reviewers found so objectionable, ostensibly on the ground that thought is nontheatrical but more profoundly from a distrust and hatred of ideas as the truly dangerous instruments of change and rehabilitation.

This is not the place for a rehearsal of the philosophic and aesthetic events that had preceded or were contemporaneous with those of the new drama—Marx's turning of bourgeois principles into the agents of their own destruction, Nietzsche's transvaluation of values, Dostoevsky's Underground Man, Rimbaud's *dérangement* in the interest of liberty, Zola's cruel realism, Cézanne's overthrow of established appearance. But it is important to keep the drama, which has a way of remaining outside the intellectual histories, from escaping into an arbitrary fate. When the theater changed it did so in obedience to a spirit that was at work everywhere; what made the plays of Ibsen and Strindberg and Shaw so disturbing was that like occurrences elsewhere in art and thought they undermined a settled conception of moral and social existence, a complacency, a system for evading truth.

But the ideas of the new drama had, of course, to discover their proper mode of existence. The first observation we make about this is, naturally, that the new plays, the masterworks of the rebellion at least, were not "ideological," not forensic, did not constitute a theater of argument. Brustein has remarked, by way of delivering a final blow to the tiresome central canon of Ibsen criticism, that he was "much less interested in specific ideas than in a generalized insight," and this was true, to one degree or another, of all the playwrights who transformed the stage. In the rehabilitation of the world and the self (the self is, ultimately, what is always dramatized, as Ibsen knew) through using thought, through that necessarily self-conscious working of a way out of illusion and sterile gestures by putting the imagination to new uses, which has been the effort of art continuously since the last century, the drama played its part according to its nature.

Bentley has demonstrated that in the plays of dramatists as diverse as Ibsen, Strindberg, Shaw, Chekhov, and Pirandello ideas— new or recovered concepts of man, of fate, experience, truth—functioned as aspects of the imagination. Ideas were incarnated in the drama, infused with feeling, made to comment upon action and indeed, the transcendently revolutionary step, made identical with action. In his discussion of how Pirandello's achievement lay not in putting forth the intellect or reason as the subject of the drama but in fusing the intellect with passion, with "action," Bentley wrote that "it is the peculiar associations of thought—with suffering and joy, with struggle and primitive fears—that is characteristic of the new drama." "Associations" is perhaps too weak a word; "impregnation" would be better.

Thought is impregnated with feeling, and feeling is in turn directed and shaped by thought. The process differs widely from playwright to playwright, but the point to be stressed here is that you cannot detach the "ideas" of Ibsen or Strindberg or even Shaw from their dramatic milieus, as academic criticism continues to do, whether it wishes to be honorific or the reverse. What distinguished these plays from those of the dead theater of their time was precisely that they were works which sought to *re-interpret* and *re-locate* man. This is a thing you naturally cannot do by simply parading the traditional passions, but you cannot do it by arguing the case either. It is in the union of dramatic imagination with philosophic intention that the triumph of the modern stage lies.

We are severely embarrassed by the word "philosophic" as applied to drama; for professional theater people it is the most damnable word they can imagine. Yet it is time for us to take Bentley's phrase and strengthen it to read "The Playwright as Philosopher," or even "as Metaphysician," since nothing better describes what modern drama is so crucially about. Let us go to a few authorities. "True poetry," Artaud writes and means true drama, "is willy-nilly metaphysical, and it is just its metaphysical bearing, I should say the intensity of its metaphysical effort, that comprises its essential worth." And Ionesco: ". . . since the artist apprehends reality directly, he is a true philosopher. And it is the broadness, the depth, the sharpness of his philosophical vision, his living philosophy, which determine his greatness."

Ionesco goes on to say that the theater "should avoid psychology, or rather give it a metaphysical dimension," and it is this action that can be traced in revolutionary drama from Ibsen on (where it was conducted within a naturalistic structure that seemed to exclude it), along with the corollary action of giving a metaphysical dimension to social existence, to struggle, to dreams, fate, and identity. The crude idea of a philosophic drama, one that *expresses* a set of ideas, is not in question here. The drama exists as an incarnation of a philosophy, a metaphysics, one that wishes to rediscover or "re-invent" man, to bring him again, in Artaud's words, "to his place between dream and events," to test him and put him under new obligations, to provide him with truer gestures and a less cowardly speech.

There is no wish here to force everything into an unyielding container, such as has been done with "absurdity," to speak only of the most current simplifying effort. The theater which has called upon a metaphysical impulse in order to resurrect itself has taken as many forms as there are minds at work in it. The metaphysical dimension of Giraudoux is very different from that of Sartre; Pirandello's does not resemble Cocteau's nor Beckett's Genet's. And there are those playwrights, such as Brecht and Shaw, for whom we have to stretch the ordinary usage of the word metaphysical to make it cover, as indeed it is meant to, concern with the nature of truth and a probing beyond appearances, since in such writers what seems to be on display is hard-headed, anti-mystical, practical thought, and insight.

But if we wish to keep the revolutionary theater from disintegrat-
ing in our minds into arbitrary fragments and accidental virtues, if
we wish to escape from the eternal sterile debate between naturalism and symbolism, poetic theater and realist theater, the epic and
the lyric—those alternatives which in our time have more to do
with details than with spirit—we need a word which will tell us
what the revolution is about. And we need it above all if we are to
understand and be capable of addressing the tremendous technical
and procedural changes that have come over drama since Ibsen first
put the practices of the boulevard and the data of the drawing-
room into the service of poetry, that poetry which Cocteau described as "of the theater" and not in it and which Artaud insisted
was, whether it considered itself to be so or not, inescapably metaphysical.

The changes undergone by plot and character transcend all others, and unite the revolutionary plays despite their differences. It
is in the altered nature of these hitherto twin pillars of the traditional idea of theater that modern drama's own metaphysical intention and aspiration are most centrally displayed. For the very
idea of character and plot rests on a concept of man and existence,
a belief in psychological coherence, in the continuity of experience
and in the permanence of what is considered to be "human nature."
When character disintegrates and plot, as "story," is abandoned, we
are witnessing the dissolution of the very concepts which underlay
their previous use.

We might say, if such terms would help, that modern drama is
existential rather than essential, that it repudiates the typologies
and narratives that an essentialist philosophy or attitude produces
from its profoundest nature. The point is that from Ibsen on drama
began to present characters who grew less and less "identifiable,"
less psychologically unified and socially coherent, less verisimilitudi-
nous. It became increasingly difficult to put oneself in the place of
the persons on stage, the dramatic and psychic energies being so
widely dispersed among the roles, the entire structure tending more
and more to resemble the relationships characteristic of poetry.
That Ibsen's last plays are usually derogated by being called loose
and symbolic is due in great part to their characters having slipped
out of their conventional moorings in psychology and personality,
to their having broken the stereotypes of action to become elements
in what, as Brustein has said, was moving toward a "drama of the
soul."

With Strindberg the process is accelerated. In the preface to *Miss*

Julie he writes, "because they are modern characters, living in a period of transition more feverishly hysterical than its predecessor at least, I have drawn my figures vacillating, disintegrated, a blend of old and new." Fourteen years later he prefaces *A Dream Play* with a much more extreme description: "The characters are split, double and multiply; they evaporate, crystallize, scatter and converge. But a single consciousness holds sway over them all—that of the dreamer." In drama a single consciousness may always have been said to have held sway over the characters—the consciousness of the playwright, who chooses, arranges, and moves things along. But what Strindberg introduced was a sovereign consciousness *within* the play itself, in which the characters participated and which might be said to have constituted the subject and action of the drama.

Participating in such a subject, the characters were no longer substitute persons, no longer identifiable by comparison or reference to figures in the world. In one way or another, with digression into various psychological or social milieus,[2] with one or another degree of emphasis on the established conflicts—the new theater has moved away from the placing on stage of surrogate figures for the audience. The culmination is with us now, in the great postwar triad of dramatists—Beckett, Ionesco, and Genet—in whose plays, otherwise so different, characters function as figments of a dramatic imagination that has passed entirely beyond psychology, beyond explanation, detection, or celebration, so that they remain free of *traits*, stuck on like labels, of personality (except in relation to one another), and of anchors in the usual conventions of history, society, or the stage itself.

As with character, so with plot, which is, of course, character in motion. Hebbel wrote that "drama should not present new stories but new relationships," and this is another mark of the drama of our time: that it has repudiated anecdote and tale. In the absence of conventional narrative the tendency is to look instead for allegory, as has happened in so much of the criticism of plays like *Waiting for Godot* or *The Blacks*. But such dramas will not yield to an allegorical interpretation, which has the effect of attempting to re-

---

[2] Even when the modern writer does go into psychological or social milieus, he is not returning to what we understand by "naturalism." The revolutionary and metaphysical impetus which is at the heart of modern drama works against verisimilitude and imitation. Pirandello's urban jousters with appearance, Giraudoux's mythic debaters, Genet's Algerian rebels, and even Ionesco's bourgeois heroes will *not* be found in the house next door.

fill the spaces that have appeared in them because of their refusal
to tell a story, their refusal to *progress.* As Jacques Guicharnaud
has written of *Godot,* "it is not an allegory, an incompleted *Pilgrim's Progress.* It is a concrete and synthetic equivalent of our
existence in the world and our consciousness of it." It is independent, entire, needing nothing from our filing cabinet of possible situations and denouements to justify itself. It *has* no situation and
reflects none; it *is* the situation itself.

For the most part drama criticism has lagged behind drama. For
a description of what has led to the creation of these plays without
heroes or histories we might more profitably turn to the writings
of a novelist like Nathalie Sarraute, to her explanations of the
changes in thought and sensibility that have resulted in the revoca-
tion of narrative and the liberation of character from the necessity
of being our reflection. She speaks of the representative new observer for whom works of art may no longer be restatements, no
matter how adroit or sincere, of the known passions and their coherent destinies. "He has seen time cease to be the swift stream that
carried the plot forward, and become a stagnant pool at the bottom
of which a slow, subtle decomposition is in progress; he has seen
our actions lose their usual motives and accepted meanings, he has
witnessed the appearance of hitherto unknown sentiments and seen
those that were most familiar change both in aspect and name."

If the drama has changed in obedience to this altered condition
of perception and knowledge, which we may consent to or resist
but which is with us nevertheless, it has been by no means a consistent, orderly, exclusive process; forms of theater overlay and jostle
one another, nothing is ever entirely replaced. The theater of character and plot continues, sometimes successfully but no longer at
the center of the dramatic imagination as it functions most acutely
today. If such theater returns as our truest drama it will in any case
be unlike its framed portraits; it too will have a metaphysical thrust,
a pressure towards escape from the airless rooms of the "lifelike"
and the recapitulated. The theater of Beckett, Ionesco, and Genet
may not extend more than a certain way into the future; but there
is no other kind of drama that seems prepared to do for us what
Artaud cried out for: a sense of life renewed, a "sense of life in
which man fearlessly makes himself master of what does not yet
exist and brings it into being."

The American theater, with its endless concentration on means
instead of ends, its cult of the actor as "expressive personality"
which so unfits him for plays in which there is no personality to

express but a condition to be exemplified, its refusal to take thought, its clinging to passion when passion is mere noise and to story when story ends in empty arrival—this theater which is our concern, our heritage, vocation, and residence, will live when it discovers and has the will to animate the narrow, fragile, dissociated, and yet, therefore, all the more revelatory existence that is the only true one the theater can have in our time. It may not happen; it has been the only wish of this essay to sketch the reasons for its not happening and the outline of the way it might.

Which Theater Is the Absurd One?

by *Edward Albee*

A theater person of my acquaintance—a man whose judgment must be respected, though more for the infallibility of his intuition than for his reasoning—remarked just the other week, "The Theater of the Absurd has had it; it's on its way out; it's through."

Now this, on the surface of it, seems to be a pretty funny attitude to be taking toward a theater movement which has, only in the past couple of years, been impressing itself on the American public consciousness. Or is it? Must we judge that a theater of such plays as Samuel Beckett's *Krapp's Last Tape*, Jean Genet's *The Balcony* (both long, long runners off-Broadway) and Eugène Ionesco's *Rhinoceros*—which, albeit in a hoked-up production, had a substantial season *on* Broadway—has been judged by the theater public and found wanting?

And shall we have to assume that The Theatre of the Absurd Repertory Company, currently [in 1962] playing at New York's Off-Broadway Cherry Lane Theatre—presenting works by Beckett, Ionesco, Genet, Arrabal, Jack Richardson, Kenneth Koch, and myself—being the first such collective representation of the movement in the United States, is also a kind of farewell to the movement? For that matter, just what *is* The Theater of the Absurd?

Well, let me come at it obliquely. When I was told, about a year ago, that I was considered a member in good standing of The Theater of the Absurd I was deeply offended. I was deeply offended because I had never heard the term before and I immediately assumed that it applied to the theater uptown—Broadway.

What (I was reasoning to myself) could be more absurd than a theater in which the esthetic criterion is something like this: A

"Which Theater is the Absurd One?" by Edward Albee. First published in *The New York Times Magazine* of February 25, 1962, and reprinted here by permission of William Morris Agency, Inc. and the author.

"good" play is one which makes money; a "bad" play (in the sense of "Naughty! Naughty!" I guess) is one which does not; a theater in which performers have plays rewritten to correspond to the public relations image of themselves; a theater in which playwrights are encouraged (what a funny word!) to think of themselves as little cogs in a great big wheel; a theater in which imitation has given way to imitation of imitation; a theater in which London "hits" are, willy-nilly, in a kind of reverse of chauvinism, greeted in a manner not unlike a colony's obeisance to the Crown; a theater in which real-estate owners and theater-party managements predetermine the success of unknown quantities; a theater in which everybody scratches and bites for billing as though it meant access to the last bomb shelter on earth; a theater in which, in a given season, there was not a single performance of a play by Beckett, Brecht, Chekhov, Genet, Ibsen, O'Casey, Pirandello, Shaw, Strindberg—or Shakespeare? What, indeed, I thought, could be more absurd than that? (My conclusions . . . obviously.)

For it emerged that The Theater of the Absurd, aside from being the title of an excellent book by Martin Esslin on what is loosely called the avant-garde theater, was a somewhat less than fortunate catch-all phrase to describe the philosophical attitudes and theater methods of a number of Europe's finest and most adventurous playwrights and their followers.

I was less offended, but still a little dubious. Simply: I don't like labels; they can be facile and can lead to non-think on the part of the public. And unless it is understood that the playwrights of The Theater of the Absurd represent a group only in the sense that they seem to be doing something of the same thing in vaguely similar ways at approximately the same time—unless this is understood, then the labeling itself will be more absurd than the label.

Playwrights, by nature, are grouchy, withdrawn, envious, greedy, suspicious and, in general, quite nice people—and the majority of them wouldn't be caught dead in a colloquy remotely resembling the following:

Ionesco. (At a Left Bank café table, spying Beckett and Genet strolling past in animated conversation.) Hey! Sam! Jean!

Genet. Hey, it's Eugene! Sam, it's Eugene!

Beckett. Well, I'll be damned. Hi there, Eugene boy.

Ionesco. Sit down, kids.

Genet. Sure thing.

Ionesco. (*Rubbing his hands together.*) Well, what's new in The
  Theater of the Absurd?
Beckett. Oh, less than a lot of people think. (*They all laugh.*)

Etc. No. Not very likely. Get a playwright alone sometime, get a
few drinks in him, and maybe he'll be persuaded to sound off about
his "intention" and the like—and hate himself for it the next day.
But put a group of playwrights together in a room, and the conversation—if there is any—will, more likely than not, concern itself with sex, restaurants, and the movies.

Very briefly, then—and reluctantly, because I am a playwright
and would much rather talk about sex, restaurants, and the movies
—and stumblingly, because I do not pretend to understand it entirely, I will try to define The Theater of the Absurd. As I get it,
The Theater of the Absurd is an absorption-in-art of certain existentialist and post-existentialist philosophical concepts having to
do, in the main, with man's attempts to make sense for himself out
of his senseless position in a world which makes no sense—which
makes no sense because the moral, religious, political, and social
structures man has erected to "illusion" himself have collapsed.

Albert Camus put it this way: "A world that can be explained
by reasoning, however faulty, is a familiar world. But in a universe
that is suddenly deprived of illusions and of light, man feels a
stranger. His is an irremediable exile, because he is deprived of
memories of a lost homeland as much as he lacks the hope of a
promised land to come. This divorce between man and his life, the
actor and his setting, truly constitutes the feeling of Absurdity."

And Eugène Ionesco says this: "Absurd is that which is devoid
of purpose. . . . Cut off from his religious, metaphysical, and tran-
scendental roots, man is lost; all his actions become senseless, absurd, useless."

And to sum up the movement, Martin Esslin writes, in his book
The Theatre of the Absurd: "Ultimately, a phenomenon like The
Theatre of the Absurd does not reflect despair or a return to dark
irrational forces but expresses modern man's endeavor to come to
terms with the world in which he lives. It attempts to make him
face up to the human condition as it really is, to free him from illusions that are bound to cause constant maladjustment and disap-
pointment. . . . For the dignity of man lies in his ability to face
reality in all its senselessness; to accept it freely, without fear, without illusions—and to laugh at it."

Amen.

(And while we're on the subject of Amen, one wearies of the complaint that The Theater of the Absurd playwrights alone are having at God these days. The notion that God is dead, indifferent, or insane—a notion blasphemous, premature, or academic depending on your persuasion—while surely a tenet of some of the playwrights under discussion, is, it seems to me, of a piece with Mr. Tennessee Williams' description of the Deity, in *The Night of the Iguana,* as "a senile delinquent.")

So much for the attempt to define terms. Now, what of this theater? What of this theater in which, for example, a legless old couple live out their lives in twin ashcans, surfacing occasionally for food or conversation (Samuel Beckett's *Endgame*); in which a man is seduced, and rather easily, by a girl with three well-formed and functioning noses (Eugène Ionesco's *Jack, or The Submission*); in which, on the same stage, one group of Negro actors is playing at pretending to be Negro (Jean Genet's *The Blacks*)?

What of this theater? Is it, as it has been accused of being, obscure, sordid, destructive, anti-theater, perverse, and absurd (in the sense of foolish)? Or is it merely, as I have so often heard it put, that, "This sort of stuff is too depressing, too . . . too mixed-up; I go to the theater to relax and have a good time."

I would submit that it is this latter attitude—that the theater is a place to relax and have a good time—in conflict with the purpose of The Theater of the Absurd—which is to make a man face up to the human condition as it really is—that has produced all the brouhaha and the dissent. I would submit that The Theater of the Absurd, in the sense that it is truly the contemporary theater, facing as it does man's condition as it is, is the Realistic theater of our time; and that the supposed Realistic theater—the term used here to mean most of what is done on Broadway—in the sense that it panders to the public need for self-congratulation and reassurance and presents a false picture of ourselves to ourselves, is, with an occasional very lovely exception, really and truly The Theater of the Absurd.

And I would submit further that the health of a nation, a society, can be determined by the art it demands. We have insisted of television and our movies that they not have anything to do with anything, that they be our never-never land; and if we demand this same function of our live theater, what will be left of the visual-auditory arts—save the dance (in which nobody talks) and music (to which nobody listens)?

It has been my fortune, the past two or three years, to travel around a good deal, in pursuit of my career—Berlin, London, Buenos Aires, for example; and I have discovered a couple of interesting things. I have discovered that audiences in these and other major cities demand of their commercial theater—and get—a season of plays in which the froth and junk are the exception and not the rule. To take a case: in Berlin, in 1959, Adamov, Genet, Beckett, and Brecht (naturally) were playing the big houses; this past fall, Beckett again, Genet again, Pinter twice, etc. To take another case: in Buenos Aires there are over a hundred experimental theaters.

These plays cannot be put on in Berlin over the head of a protesting or an indifferent audience; these experimental theaters cannot exist in Buenos Aires without subscription. In the end— and it must always come down to this, no matter what other failings a theater may have—in the end a public will get what it deserves, and no better.

I have also discovered, in my wanderings, that young people throng to what is new and fresh in the theater. Happily, this holds true in the United States as well. At the various colleges I have gone to to speak I have found an eager, friendly, and knowledgeable audience; an audience which is as dismayed by the Broadway scene as any proselytizer for the avant-garde. I have found among young people an audience which is not so preconditioned by pap as to have cut off half its responses. (It is interesting to note, by the way, that if an Off-Broadway play has a substantial run, its audiences will begin young and grow older; as the run goes on, cloth coats give way to furs, walkers and subway riders to taxi-takers. Exactly the opposite is true on Broadway.)

The young, of course, are always questioning values, knocking the status quo about, considering shibboleths to see if they are pronounceable. In time, it is to be regretted, most of them—the kids —will settle down to their own version of the easy, the standard; but in the meanwhile . . . in the meanwhile they are a wonderful, alert, alive, accepting audience.

And I would go so far as to say that it is the responsibility of everyone who pretends any interest at all in the theater to get up off their six-ninety seats and find out what the theater is *really* about. For it is a lazy public which produces a slothful and irresponsible theater.

Now, I would suspect that my theater-friend with the infallible intuition is probably right when he suggests that The Theater of the Absurd (or the avant-garde theater, or whatever you want to call it) as it now stands is on its way out. Or at least is undergoing change. All living organisms undergo constant change. And while it is certain that the nature of this theater will remain constant, its forms, its methods—its devices, if you will—most necessarily will undergo mutation.

This theater has no intention of running downhill; and the younger playwrights will make use of the immediate past and mold it to their own needs. (Harold Pinter, for example, could not have written *The Caretaker* had Samuel Beckett not existed, but Pinter is, nonetheless, moving in his own direction.) And it is my guess that the theater in the United States will always hew more closely to the post-Ibsen/Chekhov tradition than does the theater in France, let us say. It is our nature as a country, a society. But we will experiment, and we will expect your attention.

For just as it is true that our response to color and form was forever altered once the impressionist painters put their minds to canvas, it is just as true that the playwrights of The Theater of the Absurd have forever altered our response to the theater.

And one more point: The avant-garde theater is fun; it is free-swinging, bold, iconoclastic, and often wildly, wildly funny. If you will approach it with childlike innocence—putting your standard responses aside, for they do not apply—if you will approach it on its own terms, I think you will be in for a liberating surprise. I think you may no longer be content with plays that you can't remember halfway down the block. You will not only be doing yourself some good, but you will be having a great time, to boot. And even though it occurs to me that such a fine combination must be sinful, I still recommend it.

Chronology of Important Plays

Thornton Wilder (1897-   )

1931   *The Long Christmas Dinner, and other plays* (includes *Queens of France, Pullman Car Hiawatha, Love and How to Cure It, Such Things Only Happen in Books,* and *The Happy Journey to Trenton and Camden*)

1938   *Our Town*

1942   *The Skin of Our Teeth*

1954   *The Matchmaker*

Tennessee Williams (1911-   )

1944   *The Glass Menagerie*

1947   *A Streetcar Named Desire*

1948   *Summer and Smoke*

1950   *The Rose Tattoo*

1953   *Camino Real*

1954   *Cat on a Hot Tin Roof*

1957   *Orpheus Descending*

1958   *Garden District*

1960   *Period of Adjustment*

1962   *The Night of the Iguana*

1963   *The Milk Train Doesn't Stop Here Anymore*

1966   *Slapstick Tragedy*

William Inge (1913-   )

1950   *Come Back, Little Sheba*

1953   *Picnic*

1955   *Bus Stop*

1957   *The Dark at the Top of the Stairs*

1959   *A Loss of Roses*

1963   *Natural Affection*

Arthur Miller (1915-   )

1947	*All My Sons*
1949	*Death of a Salesman*
1953	*The Crucible*
1955	*A View from the Bridge*
1964	*After the Fall, Incident at Vichy*

Edward Albee (1928-   )

1958	*The Zoo Story*
1959	*The Death of Bessie Smith, The Sandbox*
1961	*The American Dream*
1962	*Who's Afraid of Virginia Woolf?*
1964	*Tiny Alice*
1966	*A Delicate Balance*

Notes on the Editor and Authors

ALVIN B. KERNAN, the editor, is Professor of English at Yale University. He is general editor of the Yale Edition of *The Plays of Ben Jonson* and has edited several Elizabethan plays. His critical writings include *The Cankered Muse, Satire of the English Renaissance* (1959), and *The Plot of Satire* (1965).

EDWARD ALBEE, the most distinguished of the younger American dramatists, has produced a number of plays in recent years, *The American Dream, Zoo Story, The Death of Bessie Smith, The Sandbox, Who's Afraid of Virginia Woolf?*, and *Tiny Alice*.

LEE BAXANDALL is an editor of *Studies on the Left*. A playwright and critic, he has written numerous articles on the modern theater. His translation of Brecht's *The Mother* was published in 1965.

TRAVIS BOGARD is Professor of English and Dramatic Art and Chairman of the Department of Dramatic Art at the University of California, Berkeley. He is the author of a critical study, *The Tragic Satire of John Webster*, published in 1955, and co-editor, with William I. Oliver, of *Modern Drama: Essays in Criticism*, published in 1965.

ROBERT BRUSTEIN is Dean of the Yale Drama School and Professor of English. An expert in Renaissance and Modern Drama, he has taught literature at Vassar and Columbia. For some years he wrote the dramatic column for *The New Republic*, and gained a reputation as a sharp but insightful critic. His book on the modern theater, *The Theater of Revolt*, was published in 1964.

TOM F. DRIVER, drama critic and Associate Professor of Christian Theology at Union Theological Seminary, is the author of *The Sense of History in Greek and Shakespearean Drama* (1960), and co-editor, with Robert Pack, of *Poems of Doubt and Belief: An anthology of modern religious poetry* (1964).

FRANCIS FERGUSSON is University Professor of Comparative Literature at Rutgers. In the opinion of many, the present editor included, Professor Fergusson is the dean of theoretical critics of the drama, and his *The Idea of a Theater* (1949) the most penetrating discussion of the nature of drama published in our century. His other works include *Dante's Drama of the Mind* (1953) and *The Human Image in Dramatic Literature* (1957).

RICHARD GILMAN, after several years as drama critic for *Commonweal*, is now serving in the same capacity for *Newsweek*. His recently published book, *Theater Today*, is a collection of his writings on the problems of the theater.

SIR TYRONE GUTHRIE is known chiefly as a director, having had a long and most distinguished career, beginning in 1924, with Sadler's Wells, The Old Vic, The Edinburgh Festival, The Shakespeare Festival Theater in Stratford, Ontario, and most recently, the Tyrone Guthrie Theater in Minneapolis. But he is also a translator and adapter of Chekhov, and the author of several influential books on the theater, the last being *In Various Directions; a View of Theatre*, published in 1965. He was knighted in 1961 and elected Chancellor of Queen's University, Belfast, in 1964.

ALLAN KAPROW began his career as a teacher of art history, but is now best known as a painter and experimenter in visual media. He has been interested for some time in producing "Happenings," and the name for this theatrical genre was taken from one of his earlier works, *18 Happenings in 6 Parts* (1959). Other works of his in this form include *Eat*, an environment; *Calling*, a happening for performers only; and *Coca Cola, Shirley Cannonball?*

ELENORE LESTER is an interested commentator on the New York theatrical scene and a shrewd observer of trends in the American drama. She is a drama critic for *The Village Voice* of New York and Assistant Professor of English at Jersey City (N.J.) State College.

GORDON ROGOFF is a contributing editor of *Tulane Drama Review* and Associate Dean of the Yale Drama School. He has been active in the American theater for some years and has recently taught drama at the New School (N.Y.). The author of numerous pieces of criticism, he is presently writing a series of articles—of which "The Juggernaut of Production," reprinted here, is one—for *TDR* that assess the general situation in the modern theater.

KENNETH TYNAN has had a distinguished career as a drama critic in England and America, writing principally for *The Observer*. He is, without question, first among public critics of the theater in the English-speaking world. The most important of his several books is *Curtains*, a collection of his drama criticism published in 1961.

Selected Bibliography

I. General Studies of American Drama

Bentley, Eric, *The Dramatic Event*, New York, 1954.
————, *In Search of Theater*, New York, 1953.
Brustein, Robert, *Seasons of Discontent*, New York, 1965.
Clurman, Harold, *Lies Like Truth; Theatre Reviews and Essays*, New York, 1958.
Cole, Toby, ed., *Playwrights on Playwriting*, New York, 1960.
Corrigan, Robert, ed., *Theater in the Twentieth Century*, New York, 1963.
Esslin, Martin, *The Theater of the Absurd*, Garden City, N.Y., 1961.
Gassner, John, *Directions in Modern Theater and Drama*, New York, 1965.
Kerr, Walter, *The Theater in Spite of Itself*, New York, 1963.
Lewis, Allan, *American Plays and Playwrights of the Contemporary Theater*, New York, 1965.
McCarthy, Mary, *Sights and Spectacles, 1937-1956*, New York, 1956.
Taubman, Howard, *The Making of the American Theater*, New York, 1965.
Tynan, Kenneth, *Curtains*, New York, 1961.
Weales, Gerald, *American Drama Since World War II*, New York, 1962.

II. Arthur Miller

Driver, Tom F., "Strength and Weakness in Arthur Miller," *Tulane Drama Review*, IV (May 1960), 45-52.
Huftel, Sheila, *Arthur Miller: The Burning Glass*, New York, 1965.
Miller, Arthur, "Tragedy and the Common Man," *New York Times* (February 27, 1949), Section II, 1 and 3.
Weales, Gerald, "Arthur Miller, Man and his Image," *Tulane Drama Review*, VII (Fall 1962), 165-80.
Welland, Denis, *Arthur Miller*, Edinburgh, 1961.

III. *Tennessee Williams*

Donahue, Francis, *The Dramatic World of Tennessee Williams,* New York, 1964.

Falk, Signi, *Tennessee Williams,* New York, 1962.

Ganz, Arthur, "The Desperate Morality of the Plays of Tennessee Williams," *American Scholar,* XXXI (Spring 1962), 278-94.

Nelson, Benjamin, *Tennessee Williams: The Man and his Work,* New York, 1961.

Popkin, Henry, "The Plays of Tennessee Williams," *Tulane Drama Review,* IV (March 1960), 45-64.

Rogoff, Gordon, "Tennessee Williams," *Tulane Drama Review,* X (Summer 1966), 78-92.

Tischler, Nancy, *Tennessee Williams, Rebellious Puritan,* New York, 1961.

IV. *William Inge*

Clurman, Harold, "A Good Play," *New Republic,* CXXII (March 13, 1950), 22-23.

Driver, Tom, "Hearts and Heads," *Christian Century,* LXXV (January 1, 1958), 17-18.

Shuman, R. Baird, *William Inge,* Twayne's United States Authors Series, New Haven, 1965.

V. *Thornton Wilder*

Burbank, Rex, *Thornton Wilder,* New York, 1961.

Fergusson, Francis, "Three Allegorists, Brecht, Wilder, and Eliot" in *The Human Image in Dramatic Literature,* New York, 1957, pp. 41-71.

Grebanier, Bernard, *Thornton Wilder,* Minneapolis, 1964.

Stephens, George, "*Our Town,* Great American Tragedy?" *Modern Drama,* I (February 1959), 258-64.

Wilder, Thornton, "Some Thoughts on Playwriting" in *The Intent of the Artist,* ed. Augusto Centeno, Princeton, 1941, pp. 83-98.

VI. *Edward Albee*

Albee, Edward, "Which Theater is the Absurd One," *New York Times Magazine* (February 25, 1962), 30-31ff.

Driver, Tom F., "What's the Matter with Edward Albee," *The Reporter,* XXX (January 2, 1964), 38-39.

Goodman, Henry, "The New Dramatists, 4: Edward Albee," *Drama Survey,* II (Spring 1962), 72-79.

VII. The Theaters

Blau, Herbert, *The Impossible Theater, a Manifesto,* New York, 1964.

Gibson, William, *The Seesaw Log; a Chronicle of the Stage Production, with the Text of* Two for the Seesaw, New York, 1959.

Guthrie, Sir Tyrone, *A New Theatre,* New York, 1964.

Hart, Moss, *Act One; an Autobiography,* New York, 1959.

Kirby, Michael, *Happenings,* New York, 1965.

Price, Julia, *The Off-Broadway Theater,* New York, 1962.

Rice, Elmer, *The Living Theater,* New York, 1959.

Strasberg, Lee, *Strasberg at the Actors Studio* (tape-recorded sessions), ed. Robert Hethman, New York, 1965.

Tulane Drama Review, X (Winter 1965) is given entirely to "Happenings." A number of critical essays on the form appear with several elaborate descriptions of various "Happenings."

American Authors in the Twentieth Century Views Series

WESTMAR COLLEGE LIBRARY